MOMPOWERMENT

Mompowerment: Insights from Successful Professional Part-time Working Moms who Balance Career and Family

Suzanne Brown

Published by Kat Biggie Press.
Columbia, SC 29229
http://katbiggiepress.com

Cover design by Lilah Higgins
Book design Write.Publish.Sell
Edited by Betsy Rhame-Minor

ISBN-13: 978-0-9899347-9-4
Library of Congress Control Number: 2017948403
First Edition: September 2017

10 9 8 7 6 5 4 3 2 1

DEDICATION

To all the moms out there who are trying to have more work-life balance.

CONTENTS

INTRODUCTION

I HAD NO IDEA what I was getting myself in to when I started reaching out to moms to hear their stories. It didn't really occur to me what I was asking moms to share. And, thankfully, the moms I spoke with shared a lot. Their stories were full of information on aspects of their roles and overall career, but the stories were also very personal. Moms shared their motivation, which wasn't always because of something fun or light. They were dealing with divorces and children's development delays. There was stress from full-time jobs that was so bad that it made some of the moms literally sick. One by one, these women opened up their lives, answering my questions, sharing lessons they learned and successes they've had, so other moms can benefit.

And, on this amazing journey, I have personally learned so much from these stories and all the advice, insights, and challenges. These moms have pushed me to think differently about my own approach to being a professional part-time working mom. I've even integrated tips and advice I heard from other moms in my own life, and I had been working part-time for almost a year when I started interviewing moms for the book.

I know that when you look for advice on your career as a working mom, there is plenty out there. And much of it is designed to help you be that much more amazing and successful in your career. I set out to write a different kind of book. I wanted to help moms define success in their own terms and, for some, that means working part time. There are few, if any, places to go to learn about being successful as a professional part-time working mom.

The reality is that you can find all sorts of information on the moms who lean in and the moms who have opted out.[1] You can even find information on the moms who opted out in the early 2000s and realized ten years later that they might have originally taken a different approach, now that they started trying to opt in again.[2]

A lawyer who works in Chicago about thirty hours per week talked about these opt-out moms trying to opt back in. She knows women from this group. And she describes some of them as feeling a bit lost as they overcame challenges on their path to reentering the business world after a long stretch away. And those kinds of conversations pushed me to keep going on my journey.

The more I talked to moms I know who have chosen not to work while having young kids at home, and the more I read, the more determined I became to finish the interviews and write this book. So many moms I know and read about walked away from their careers because they couldn't find the right combination or balance of working and being the mom they wanted to be. The more I spoke with my friends with demanding full-time jobs who said they simply couldn't do their roles part time, the more interested I became in interviewing women in all sorts of fields.

And this is what I discovered: being a professional part-time working mom is doable. It's not only doable, but moms can use the part-time approach to their careers and still be successful – incredibly successful. And they get the benefit of more time with family and being the mom they want to be. The women who shared their stories didn't have to choose and neither do you (unless you want to).

You might be asking what will you get out of reading this book versus others? The book is designed to be informative and, in some ways, a reference book. Use it to help you transition to a professional part-time role and figure out solutions to challenges you may face on your path. You might even read this book more than once.

And, while the lens I use to write this book is that of a mom, anyone interested in a professional part-time role can pick up this book and find useful information. You could be a Baby Boomer interested in partially retiring or a professional part-time working dad (I've had part-time working dads specifically reach out to me, so there just might be a version dedicated specifically to them one day). Or you might be a Millennial who doesn't have kids or even plan to, but wants to strike your ideal work-life balance. There will be more for those audiences on the blog and in future writing. For now, I write in the voice of a mom and for moms, because that is my lens. It's what I know and who I see in the mirror each day.

Perhaps you're reading this book as you think about your career path before entering graduate school. It could be helpful to think through the aspects I mention about industry and what companies offer, even before you choose a company to work for. This is especially important if you'd like to stay in an industry or at a company long-term.

Maybe you're about to have your first child. While there are books on how to make the most of maternity leave and on how to be amazing once you return from maternity leave to your same job, what about the moms who decide they might want to have a different career approach when they get back? That is one way to look at the information in this book.

You might be reading or even rereading this book with the birth of your second child, when juggling a career and home life becomes that much more complex. And you may read the advice and suggestions differently when you're juggling more things.

You will see that each chapter has a summary at the end. If there is a chapter with information that you feel very confident about and you might want to skip it, take a look at the summary to see if there is anything you still might want to check out in that specific chapter.

So as you read this and wonder about the transition to a professional part-time role as a mom, I ask you to consider what might be holding you back from making this change. My hope is that in these pages, you find ways to overcome the challenges that you fear and that hold you back. And you will create a situation where you feel empowered in career and motherhood.

You won't have to figure things out alone. I'm here with you on your journey. I'll help you uncover how you can have the life you want that combines career and family the way you want. You will get tools that will help you think differently about your career approach.

To help, I share exercises throughout the book, but I also share free tools such as templates and worksheets for you to download at www.mompowerment.com/booktemplates.

My biggest hope is that you find this information useful and that it helps you on your path to figuring out what works for you and your family. Enjoy!

PART I:

AN INTRODUCTION TO THE PROFESSIONAL PART-TIME WORKING MOM

CHAPTER 1:

YOU ARE NOT ALONE

Where Are All the Stories?

You're a full-time working mom who loves her career. The fifty or more hours per week is getting old though, even for someone who loves her job. Your child had a rough night last night because he's teething, and you have to send him to daycare when you really want to curl up and cuddle, comforting him. Instead, you head to work, feeling sleep deprived, dreading the meetings on your calendar. How can you focus on work when you'll be thinking about your little boy and how he's miserable right now?

You're realizing you need to spend more time focusing on your child. You weren't fully prepared when the pediatrician started talking about your son's developmental delay. You thought something was a bit off, but this is another level. Your mother has offered to take him to speech therapy, but you want to be the one to do it. It's a few times a week though, and your manager has already been pushing back when you ask to leave early or come in late. What will your manager say now? Will you be able to go to these important sessions multiple times a week or do you need to quit your job? Does it really have to get to that point?

Your daughter is now a preteen and is having a rough go, because that happens at this age. (Although challenging moments happen at any age, right?) You're finding yourself wanting to be around more, but how can that happen with your full-time job? Could you figure out a way to be more available to your daughter and stay engaged at work? How can you make that happen?

You've noticed your parents are having more health issues as illnesses linger and they deal with more and more aches and pains. What will you do if they need more of your attention when you're already squeezed between your own family obligations and work? How can you fit more into your already busy day?

What happens when you get back from maternity leave? You love sitting and simply holding your child. And that baby smell! How are you going to hand your baby to someone else for eight or ten hours each and every day? Maybe you won't go back to work once maternity leave is over. Are you ready to leave the workforce? For how long? You love your job.

You're trying to be the best mom, wife, employee, friend, sibling, daughter, and everything else that you can. It's getting harder and harder though. If only you could create more flexibility in the next few years to be more engaged with your family.

Do any of these sound like your own story? Each story is from a mom I interviewed or have since spoken with. These aren't unusual situations for moms though.

I get it. We all get it. Motherhood is rewarding, amazing, magical, and all things incredible. Let's face it being a mom is also hard. Being a full-time working mom with a career, maybe even a demanding career, is even more challenging. You're not alone in feeling this pull to be engaged in your child's life and yet you don't want to walk away from your career.

The Not-so-small Club of Moms Who Want to Work Part Time

I said you're not alone and that's putting it mildly. Statistics show you're not alone in feeling the desire for less time at work and more time with family. A Pew Research poll shows that almost half of moms, 47 percent, want to work part-time.[1] When you break it down, about 44 percent of full-time working moms (FTWMs) and 40 percent of stay-at-home moms (SAHMs) say part time would be their ideal situation.[2] Even though almost half of moms would like to work part time, fewer than 17 percent of moms do.[3]

Mind the Gap

Some moms are happy as FTWMs, which is good for their situations. Some want to be SAHMs and that works for them. And some moms are SAHMs or FTWMs because they feel they must choose one or the other. Why don't more moms choose part-time work if so many want that approach to their careers? Essentially, why is there such a large gap between the moms who want to work part time and the moms that do? What is it about that area of gray in between SAHM and FTWM? I have a few theories on why more moms don't choose the professional part-time approach.

I Have Two Choices, SAHM or FTWM, Right?

Look around for stories on professional part-time working moms (PPWMs). I looked because I wanted a place to point people who were asking me how I make it work. I figured there must be a place where moms can read more about this work approach. I was wrong. I didn't find consistent resources and I looked everywhere. That lack of information and success stories about PPWMs can lead to some moms choosing between what they believe are their only two options: SAHM and FTWM. They don't understand the other option out there because there isn't information easily available. It's almost like it's hidden or a secret. Moms interested in this option don't know where to go to find information to feel empowered to make this choice and set themselves up for success.

And, on the flip side, PPWMs don't know other moms are looking for information or don't know where to share their stories. The moms

I interviewed, more than 110 total, said over and over that they were glad someone is finally putting together a resource to get the word out and create a place to start sharing stories and ideas. They shared they wished this resource was available when they started down their own path that eventually led them to the PPWM career model.

I Don't Want a Part-time Job, Do I?

There is another challenge when it comes to researching professional part-time work opportunities for moms. When you hear the term "part-time work," you might think of lower-paying services and retail types of roles, or even seasonal employment. Don't get me wrong, these roles are vital to the economy and often bring in money that is integral to a family budget. If you're mid-level or senior-level at a company, these seasonal and more traditionally known part-time roles are probably not where you want to be. And if that's all you know about or find for part-time work, you're likely not looking at part-time as a potential career approach.

Where Can I Find Professional Part-time Work?

My final thought on what makes working moms choose is that there aren't a lot of job postings for professional part-time work. If you search online for the term "part-time," it's generally about the lower-paying roles I mentioned. Larger companies don't tend to list these types of roles on their websites. And that only deters moms and women from going down the path of looking for part-time work opportunities or creating them in the companies where they currently work. It is hard to find these if you're going the traditional route of finding a new role. And you might think that if you can't find them, then professional part-time roles probably don't exist.

More Sharing Can Lead to Fewer Women Leaving the Workforce

Imagine the number of mothers who leave the workforce to care for their children and other family obligations because they didn't know about the professional part-time career model. Could talking about and creating more part-time career opportunities keep more moms in the workforce or bring moms back to the workforce? The interviews I conducted and conversations I've had lead me to believe the answer is a resounding "Yes!" It won't lead to all previously FTWMs who became SAHMs coming back to the workforce, but some will. And maybe those moms who work full time will stay in the workforce instead of leave to care for family. And, we need moms and women in the workforce for a variety of reasons. (I'll share more about this specifically in Chapter 11.)

Definition of a PPWM

As you're reading this, you might be wondering, what is a PPWM anyway? How many hours are they working and what types of roles do they have? What industries are they in?

How Many Hours Does She Work?

For this book and for all things Mompowerment, a PPWM is engaged in her career and is considered a professional of some sort, but she works less than her colleagues or the industry norm. That is the basic difference.

The moms worked as few as five hours a week and as many as forty. You may be wondering how forty hours per week can be considered part time. It's relative. When you compare forty hours to colleagues working sixty or more, forty is part time. The number of hours will depend on the industry or even the company norm.

What Industry Does She Work In?

These moms aren't in special industries or locations. There isn't a specific industry in which all the moms work. Being a PPWM can happen in all sorts of careers and industries, such as financial services, education, consulting, medicine, engineering, accounting, marketing, nonprofits, and beauty, to name a few.

Tell Me About Her Experience

There are PPWMs at all levels, although the women I spoke with tended to be more seasoned and have more experience. These moms worked an average of nine years before transitioning to a part-time role, which they've been in an average of about five years.

About 62 percent of the moms work for a company, both large and small businesses. The other roughly 38 percent are entrepreneurs (or "mompreneurs," if you prefer) who started their own business.

Whether they work for someone else or work for themselves, these women are seasoned professionals with years of experience. They know their own strengths and understand what they bring to the table. They are often in leadership positions, though not always the team lead, and are decision-makers.

Where Does She Live?

The moms are all over the United States, so it's not about certain regions of the country. Most moms I interviewed are in larger cities or the surrounding suburbs (about 96 percent). The rest either work for themselves or have a work-from-home situation with their employer. This is not meant to discourage moms who want professional part-time opportunities in smaller towns, away from large cities. It might mean that you need to create your part-time opportunity or be creative in structuring a role within a company.

How Did She Find Part-time Work?

The question I often get is where to find these roles. They're not usually listed in easily accessible places online, although there are some websites dedicated to these types of roles (see more on www. mompowerment.com). About 30 percent of the moms I interviewed, or almost half of those who are employed by a company, found their current role outside of their then current employer. The other half of those employed part-time working moms usually negotiated to transition their current role into a part-time role. There were a few moms who created their position at their current employer, so it's a new role for them and the company.

Are There Differences in How the Moms Interviewed Approach their Careers?

When I analyzed the interviews, most of the moms fell into one of three groups: High Performing Go-Getter, Mellowed Achiever, and Engaged and Relevant. Not even a handful described a situation where they were completely disengaged from career and simply going through the motions at work. Let's look into each of these three groups.

High Performing Go-Getter

These moms are still highly engaged in their careers. Many of these women are still integral members of their team. Some did their full workload in fewer hours. Some were still being promoted. And some transitioned to part time for a specific amount of time, with the specific intention of going back to work full time in the near or distant future. If they were entrepreneurs, it was because they realized they could work fewer hours and make the same or more money. As entrepreneurs, they had highly sought after skills and/or knowledge. These moms made the most of their time at work and were highly engaged with family when at home.

Mellowed Achiever

These moms at one point had likely been High Performing Go Getters, but they were moving their focus away from work to family, at least for now. They still want to do a good job, but they weren't necessarily looking for promotion and taking on new responsibility. Some downshifted from High Performing Go Getter to this group because they were burned out, especially with the added pressure of motherhood. Others used their transition to professional part-time work to pivot their careers to something they were more passionate about, but took their time to make that happen. The employed moms were very specific about their boundaries at work, so they could enjoy their time with family when they were away from work. The entrepreneurs within this group started their own business to have more control over their schedule and/or more balance in their lives.

Engaged and Relevant

These moms shared that family was their focus. It was *that* simple. These moms realized they didn't want to step out of the workforce because reentering is hard. They weren't trying to get to the next level, at least at this moment in their lives, and they were OK with that. Part of why they stayed in the workforce was to make extra income for the family and/or to have a social outlet with adults. These moms didn't seem as sure about going back full time down the road.

In summary:

There is no specific type of industry, location, or type of role in which most PPWMs can be found.

- If you want to be a PPWM, you're not alone.

- PPWMs work in all sorts of industries and roles across the United States.
- The number of hours that part-time moms work generally depends on the company and industry.
- Part-time work can range from five to forty hours per week (compared to sixty or more per week).
- There are plenty of opportunities to find part-time professional opportunities at companies, both large and small.
- Some moms created a new position at their current employer.
- The moms interviewed seemed to be in one of three groups: High Performing Go-Getter, Mellow Achiever, and Engaged and Relevant.

CHAPTER 2:

WHY NOW?

YOU MIGHT BE WONDERING why I decided to write this book now. Granted, it took a while – three years – to interview 110 PPWMs while working in my own professional part-time role. There is more to it though. It seems like we're at a turning point. Companies, leadership, and even government are finally talking about aspects of the workplace that impact working moms in the United States. Additionally, more and more conversations are happening about work-life balance and the positive impact it has on employees at the office and at home.

Maternity Leave and Then What?

At the time that this was written, the conversation was finally starting in companies and even at some levels of government on the topic of maternity leave. An increasing number of companies are starting to offer paid time off for moms to spend weeks or even months with their newborns and allow their bodies to recuperate from giving birth. A recent study by the Society of Human Resource Management and Families at Work Institute polled 899 businesses across the United States. They found that, "Overall, 75 percent of employers with 50 or more employees provide 12 or more weeks of maternity leave."[1] About 58 percent of companies offer some level of paid maternity leave.[2]

What happens after those two, three, or even six months of maternity leave? Interestingly, this is in comparison to three to twelve months or more of paid leave in other developed countries.[3]

We're hearing more about maternity leave, but what about the early development years of childhood? Studies show the importance of this young age —years two through four — in a child's development. A Harvard study explains how the pathways that develop in the brain in these early years impact lifelong "learning, behavior, and health."[4] The emotional foundation is formed at this stage as well.[5] So much is happening at this moment in a child's development and some moms want to miss as little as possible. How can they though, if they're working full time, especially in demanding jobs that don't allow for a lot of time with family?

What about Moms of Older Kids?

How do moms stay or get involved in the lives of their older children who might have activities where they practice and compete after school and on weekends? What about moms simply being available to their kids, who need guidance during the preteen or teenage years? Several of the moms shared that their older children needed mom to be around even more, to go from one place to another or for encouragement during these sometimes tough years in a child's development.

For FTWMs, the answer is that they usually don't get that involved in their kids' activities and provide whatever support they can at dinner, bedtime, or on the weekends. And, these moms can make themselves available during the day, most of the time, if their children need to get a hold of them.

Perhaps their company might provide some flexibility and allow for leaving early to participate in a special lunch at their child's school or to attend their child's performance or sporting event. For many though, those are rare occasions and the moms miss various opportunities to support their children by showing up and cheering them on regularly. The moms, who are frequent participants and cheerleaders, then work for hours after the kids are in bed to catch up on work.

Moms are Getting Sandwiched

Caring for children is not the only challenge that moms are facing when it comes to taking care of their families. At the time that this book was written, consider that roughly 10,000 Baby Boomers turn retirement age every day, which will continue for at least a decade.[6] Who will care for this aging population? In many households, the duties of childcare *and* caring for parents/parents in-law fall to moms.

This is something that women are trying to change, but for now, those duties fall mainly on moms' shoulders. Moms are essentially getting sandwiched and their time is getting squeezed between caring for their children and their parents or in-laws, on top of trying to manage their careers. They can't stop being moms to their kids and can't stop being daughters or daughters-in-law, but they can stop being employees, and that is what some will or already do.

An education consultant in the Atlanta area works ten to fifteen hours per week and is currently working on a doctorate in education to achieve her long-term goal of being a part-time professor. She and her husband recently bought a house big enough for their family of four and for both sets of grandparents to move in. She understands that she and her husband will be caring for both sets of parents over time. She wants to be fulfilled professionally and spend time with her family, so she's laying the foundation to achieve that.

Educated Women are Waiting to Have Children

I want to cover this next topic because it impacts women's long-term career trajectory. According to a Pew Research study, educated women in the United States are having babies later in life. About 40 percent of women with an undergraduate degree and 54 percent of women with a master degree have babies at age 30 or older, which is four years older than the U.S. average of 26.[7]

I'm one of these women. I had our older son when I was 35 and our younger son when I was 38. I also understand that my husband and I were fortunate in our experience with getting pregnant quickly. That's not the case for everyone.

I spoke with a doctor of obstetrics and gynecology (OB-GYN) in Austin, Texas, who works thirty to forty hours per week (in comparison to her fellow partners, who work sixty or more), and it was a fascinating interview. She made an interesting statement that stuck with me, stating simply that "Women can't always have babies." Alongside her patients, she deals with this challenge and heartbreak of infertility every day. I'm not looking to create controversy because of her statement. I mention this because, as women continue to delay having babies, often for career, it can become harder for them to conceive when they are ready to turn their attention to family.

Even with fertility treatments, some women still struggle to have children. And it's not uncommon for women to have infertility challenges. About 12 percent of women of child-bearing age have been treated for infertility and it impacts about one in eight married couples.[8]

We assume that when we're ready to have children that our bodies will cooperate with us. The reality is that isn't always the case. There are all sorts of ways that women overcome infertility challenges. Women I interviewed and even friends have done in vitro fertilization (IVF), sometimes multiple rounds of it. Women can freeze their eggs or even use an egg donor. You probably know women who have done at least one of these. However, these options aren't a guarantee that women can have children later in life.

What happens if women wait too long and they can't have children, even with the fertility treatments and ever-changing science available? And, the reality is that this challenge isn't only age-based. Some of the women who shared their stories with me had fertility challenges from the beginning of trying to conceive — in their mid-twenties. It was part of what led them to have a part-time approach to career once they finally had children.

For some women who want to become mothers, IVF does work. A few decided to adopt. Some women find alternate options like surrogacy. Others still decide that children are not in their future and their lives are already complete (I know more and more women who feel this way).

The right scenario varies from woman to woman, couple to couple, or family to family. Only you will know the right solution for you and your situation, and there shouldn't be pressure to go one way based on what you see around you.

I'm not sharing this as a scare tactic to get women to have babies right out of college or to give up their desire to be a mom if they choose to wait. It's important to live your life as you choose based on what you want and need. Setting personal and career goals that you strive to achieve is a natural approach to life for many, especially high-performing women, one which I understand and did myself.

With these potential fertility issues in mind, I am offering a different approach for women to consider as an option. The OB-GYN who I spoke with suggested that "women can integrate children into their career approach instead of *after* reaching their career goals." Her recommended approach is for women to keep their demanding careers on track or get them back on track after having children. And a way to have children while having a demanding role is to use the part-time career model.

It turns out that her recommendation, based on her own experience and that of her patients, is in line with data from a Pew Research study. When asked about how family impacts career, 59 percent of moms said it has no impact.[9] That doesn't mean that being a working mother is easy, but it also doesn't mean your career immediately shuts down once you have kids.

Transitioning to a professional part-time role allows moms to stay on their career trajectory instead of walking away from a career outright. Moms don't have to *choose* between career and family along the path. You can work *and* be the engaged mother you want to be. You *can* be successful in this career model in a job you enjoy. Having a demanding and rewarding career *and* being involved in the lives of your children to the level that you want is doable. These roles aren't everywhere you look, but they are available and you can make them happen, even in situations that don't seem to support it at first glance.

In summary:

Changes are happening that impact women and moms in the U.S. workforce.

- More companies are starting to offer paid maternity leave, but what about moms wanting to stay engaged during the extremely important early development years?
- What about the moms with older children who need more support from mom to go from place to place or to provide more personal support?
- What about moms whose work might be impacted by adding the care of aging Baby Boomer parents and in-laws?
- Educated women are having babies later in life, which can negatively impact their fertility chances.
- Consider having children while keeping your career on track.

CHAPTER 3:

BENEFITS OF PROFESSIONAL PART-TIME ROLES

NOT LONG AGO, I had a conversation with a friend who asked me what I get out of having a reduced work schedule. As we talked more, I realized she was asking about the benefit of transitioning to a part-time role. So, what is the benefit to transitioning to a professional part-time role?

Going from full time to part time doesn't make everything easy, but it can make aspects of the combination of work and the personal side of things easier. And for many moms who shared their story, they were able to be more of the moms they wanted to be. For starters, the number one benefit I heard in interviews was time with family, whether attending activities or simply being home for dinner. (Not to mention time to make a healthy dinner.) The OB-GYN in Austin, Texas, shared "As a working mom, I can be a good wife or mom or doctor, but it's hard to do all three well." When she shifted to a job share situation (more on that in Chapter 9) in which she works part time, she describes how she reclaimed part of her life. And, as she put it, "it's never perfect, but it's doable."

In my case, I returned from maternity leave and immediately started working part time in the large marketing agency where I had worked for about five and a half years. My sights were set on being an engaged mom long-term and missing as little as possible during those early years. I eventually wanted to be involved with his school once he was in preschool, so that I could be part of the fun activities and engage with his teachers. In the short-term, I wanted to attend mother and baby classes for things like music. That wouldn't be possible with a full-time role. Not too long after our older son's first birthday, I transitioned to working for myself. I had more control over my schedule and could truly be the mom I wanted to be, adjusting workload and types of work based on my needs and those of my family.

A freelance technical writer in Colorado, who works about thirty hours per week, explained the benefit of working part time in a way that most moms can relate to. She said, "There is a lot more saying 'yes' to my kids. . . . I wonder how many times I had to say 'no' [in the past]." A sentiment, which came up over and over was articulated by a social work supervisor, who is based out of Michigan and works about twenty hours per week: "It makes me a better wife and better mom."

Moms who I talked to shared that there was little time to do stuff when they worked full time. There was the rush to pick up kids after work, quickly prepare and then eat dinner, help with homework, bathe kids or clean up the kitchen while older kids bathed, and then get kids ready for bed. And by that point, most moms were exhausted, especially after a full day of work. (I'm tired just thinking about it.)

Weekends were a time to catch up and do the things that weren't done during the week, such as dropping off and picking up dry cleaning, doing grocery shopping, and cleaning the house. There might have been kids' activities such as games or competitions. And there was even the need to help kids with projects.

Moms shared much of the time as a family was getting things done, instead of enjoying the moment. When was there time to even be able to create the moments as a family before these moms transitioned to professional part-time roles? When was there time to say "yes" to family fun?

Spending time together as a family is what matters, right? We all want to create and enjoy the moments together, not work so hard and ultimately fly through them. Can you relate? Is this what you're going through now? A part-time role doesn't magically make everything better as a parent, but it can help you get more of what you want.

Saying Yes to More Family Time

The number one benefit of working part time was more time with family. More than half of moms talked about this specifically. They had time to pick kids up from school or meet the bus. They took kids to practice and attended events regularly. These moms often knew their kids' friends well and were around to provide support during challenging moments for their kids. They went to standing appointments and took care of sick kids. Moms talked about this benefit in so many ways.

What about Balance?

Let's talk about balance for a moment, since it's the topic I get the most questions about from moms interested in transitioning to a professional part-time role. About a quarter of moms mentioned balance as an end benefit. It seemed more like moms used balance to get more of what they wanted, especially time with kids. They didn't necessarily use balance as an end benefit in many cases, even when they mentioned the concept in our conversations.

Working part time allows you more of the work-life balance you crave. You can do some of the stuff reserved for weekends (e.g., errands or chores) during the week. It gives you a chance to engage in different ways with your kids and your career, so you get the life you want.

The concept of balance is interesting and somewhat tricky. It's not something you can check off a list. You can't set it once and it's done. It's a constant shift in priorities — in your priorities — not those of anyone else. It looks different for each of us and that's OK.

I think of balance as more of a constantly moving pendulum that sways between work and family. Some days it swings more toward work and other days it's closer to family. It's constantly moving for me. Most moms I spoke with alluded to this shifting as well. The reality is that there is never (or almost never) a perfect balance between family and work, which is natural and reasonable. Moms shouldn't be striving for something that is near impossible to achieve daily. If you look at balance over time it's more realistic. And it sets a new way to think about it, which might help with the mommy guilt and overall pressure of trying to achieve daily balance.

More Flexibility

Moms shared all sorts of benefits to working part time in their interviews. A key benefit shared during the interviews was flexibility. A college counselor at a high school in Austin, Texas, who works about twenty hours per week, described what flexibility does for her: "My part-time role allows me the flexibility to be more productive with my day. I can stay some afternoons when I need to or take days off when needed."

Part of what allowed for flexibility was more control over their schedules. Many moms shared this was part of why they transitioned. They were able to spend more time with kids because they controlled when their workday ended or which days they were in the office.

More Satisfaction

For other moms I interviewed, the benefit of working part time was the opportunity to feel more satisfaction in all areas of their lives. A graphic designer in Cody, Wyoming, who works for herself about twenty hours a week, shared, "I have the freedom to live life how I want. I get to decide."

Several moms discussed being satisfied with their business achievements because it wasn't only about motherhood. These moms described feeling empowered to make decisions and attain goals in areas that had nothing to do with their children. I'm a strong believer that I enable my children to attain goals, but their achievements aren't mine. I need to continue to accomplish my own goals to be fulfilled. Many of these moms who talked about satisfaction had that same perspective. As a mom, who works ten to twenty hours per week in fundraising for a social work organization in Westchester County, New York, shared, "I got my life back" when she went to a part-time schedule. She said simply, "I'm not a slave to my job anymore."

Many moms also felt less stress as a result of transitioning to a part-time role, so there was more room for satisfaction and less room for stress. And that might also be a by-product of simply having more time to get things done.

Financial Contribution

No question, there is a financial aspect to working part time. Moms mentioned being able to contribute financially in many interviews. Part of it was to provide more income for their families to ensure their family's lifestyle was maintained, whether for private schools or paying for vacation and activities for kids. For others, it was to feel more financially independent.

One mom had a very different perspective, which reframed her contribution to her family's bottom line. The part-time preschool teacher, who works about fifteen hours a week, said, "My salary covers the mortgage." Instead of looking at her salary as the extra stuff, this mom wants her salary to cover one of the most important things for her family. It makes her salary much more important in the eyes of her family.

Learning New Skills

Learning a new skill or furthering their education came up a few times as a benefit to working part time. One physician, who works twenty-five to thirty hours per week in Austin, Texas, used her extra time to get a holistic and integrative medicine certificate, a long-time area of interest. She wanted that additional education so she could think differently about patient care.

"I'm still building skills. This is the second part of my life and career," shared a mom, who currently works in media sales for a local publication in Austin, Texas, for about fifteen hours each week. Her part-time role enabled her to get certified to teach yoga when she realized her area of interest is yoga therapy and health and wellness. This mom wouldn't have the opportunity to learn this new skill if she had been in her full-time technology role. She took advantage of the hours and the income from her part-time job to help her pivot into a second career when she wasn't caring for kids or working part time.

Motherhood and Personal Identity

A benefit of working part time near and dear to my heart and to so many women I know personally is that of work providing an identity away from family. While we all love our families and truly enjoy the time we spend with our children and significant other, we need our own identity. So many moms I interviewed talked about this, which isn't surprising with high performers.

When I became a mother, the first year was so overwhelming. We were focused on our baby and almost nothing else, or that's how it felt. I remember waking up one morning around the time our older son turned one, looking in the mirror, and wondering what happened. Where had I gone? The woman I describe as before kids was different than the woman now looking at me in the mirror. I had been working part time for a large company at the time. I was trying to get through each day, not aiming to set goals for myself or trying to use my own natural rhythms. I was focusing on being a mom and the rest of me was temporarily lost.

This happened again, to a much lesser extent, when we had our younger son. The transition to two was incredibly tough in our house as we had a spirited, strong-willed toddler plus a newborn. This time I was working for myself, so I stepped away from my business for a few months to focus on our children and then came back to client work, ready to make things happen. Plus, I had a book to work on that I was excited about. I knew I didn't want to wake up one morning a year into having two children, wondering what happened yet again.

Getting back to work helped with my own personal identity. I wanted to be more than a mom. I was (and still am) a mom, wife, writer, consultant, researcher, thought provoker, and so much more. I felt re-energized and stimulated mentally, even though I was exhausted physically. That something else is what kept me engaged in all areas of my life. It made me a better mom because I was confident and fulfilled in all the areas of my life.

I'm not alone in losing myself in motherhood and not focusing on my needs. Some of the moms I spoke with initially walked away from their careers and became SAHMs for a short time or even for years. For some of these SAHMs, they went back to work to regain their identity. A writer in the nonprofit sector in the Boston area, who works twenty-five to thirty hours per week, shared that she needed the professional side of things to feel like she had her own identity again.

Part-time Schedules and Passion Projects

The subject of passion projects came up over and over. This was interesting, since only a handful of moms talked about the specific benefit of being able to work on passion projects with a part-time schedule. Since it was an indirect benefit though, I wanted to mention it.

For some moms, these passion projects are an outlet. An information technology consultant in the beverage industry, who now works about twenty to twenty-five hours per week, had a very demanding job before transitioning to a part-time approach to her career. At one point, while still working full-time, she even had to cancel a family vacation because of work demands. Now, in addition to more time with her own family, she has time to help families on their path to adoption. As the mother of adopted children, she feels passionately about helping other families on their adoption journey.

For others, these passion projects turn into a business over time. A director of digital marketing in New York City has been working part time at about twenty to thirty hours per week for more than seven years. A few years ago, she started her own coaching business and is reducing her time in her part-time job so that she can build her coaching practice. She has flexibility and can balance her marketing work, build her coaching business, and continue to be the primary caregiver for her family. In the long run though, she'll focus on a business she is truly passionate about. How long would it have taken her to make this happen if she had been in a full-time role? Would she even have pursued this new passion if she had been working full time?

A woman's wellness coach, who helps moms figure out their own self-care needs, was a SAHM for about ten years. She had received a doctorate before taking time off when her first child was born. When her youngest of five children turned two, this self-care coach started getting antsy about going back to work. She started to think through what she wanted to do and found "her calling," as she describes it.

Being a Better Partner

Several moms talked about one benefit of working part-time is removing pressure from their significant other. When there is more than one income in the house, both parents deal with less financial pressure.

Some moms even describe the opportunity to work part-time as helping their significant other feel less trapped in their role.

A marketing consultant in the Los Angeles area, who works for herself about thirty-five to forty hours per week, described moving into a part-time role instead of staying at home as an opportunity for her husband to "pursue his huge potential." Had she become a SAHM, her husband would have remained in his job instead of being able to pursue a master degree and change careers.

Benefit for Family

I was surprised by the many moms who talked about how these benefits trickled down to their families. The moms' flexibility impacted their kids. Maintaining their own identity made them better moms. Families benefitted from the moms' efforts on many levels, both directly and indirectly.

We don't talk about this aspect enough as PPWMs. I wanted to make sure to share this idea from the interviews, especially since there are statistics to back this up.

It turns out that about 59 percent of Americans think that one parent in a two-parent household should stay home to care for children, according to a 2016 Pew Research study.[1] The parent who stays home is usually the mother, although more dads are taking on this role, and more and more households have moms as the primary breadwinner. In case you're wondering, about 29 percent of partnered women are breadwinners in their families, according to a 2015 study done by Working Mother Research Institute.[2]

Although many Americans agree with this concept, a worldwide study shows it might be better for moms to work, including in part-time roles.[3] More than 13,000 women were part of this research, which found that daughters of working moms, whether part time or full time, do better in the workforce over the long-term.[4] These daughters are more likely to have jobs, earn a higher wage and have supervisory roles versus daughters of SAHMs.[5]

The same study with more than 13,000 women included more than 18,000 men and the impact on sons was different than that on daughters.[6] Men whose mothers worked, whether part time or full time, are more likely to spend more time on family care duties than those whose mothers stayed at home.[7]

These findings may seem surprising, given so many Americans think moms should stay at home for the benefit of their children.

Part-time Working Moms Are Happier

There is an old saying that "If momma's not happy, no one's happy." Being happier came up over and over in my conversations. I heard consistent comments about when moms are happier, everyone in the family is also generally happier and their quality of life improved. And this is something that is incredibly important in the long-term for the moms and their families. And as moms shared they often felt less stress, that probably allowed for more time for happiness as well, right?

It turns out that "married mothers who are able to cut back at work to accommodate their family's needs tend to be happier."[8] A Pew Research study shares that part-time working moms are more likely to take the juggling act in stride and they seem more likely to attain the right level of time with kids and their significant other, which is not too little *and* not too much.[9]

In summary:

Although transitioning to a professional part-time role doesn't make everything easy for moms, it can help you get more of what you're looking for.

- Moms in interviews mentioned more time with family,

flexibility, balance, less stress, ability to establish or re-establish a personal identity, and being able to contribute financially, to name a few.

- Families, not only moms, benefit from the transition to part-time work roles.
- There is a long-term benefit to daughters and sons whose moms work.
- Part-time working moms are happier than both FTWMs and SAHMs.

PART II:
HOW TO KNOW IF A PROFESSIONAL PART-TIME ROLE IS RIGHT FOR YOU

CASE STUDY: What Happens when Life at Home Changes

The Atlanta-based information technology (IT) consultant had worked for sixteen years in various operations roles in media companies and somewhere in there, took a break to do a two-year MBA. Her roles within the media industry were demanding; so much so that at one point, she had to cancel a family vacation. And that led her to consider other industries.

She found a great role at a major beverage company, but things at home changed. The IT professional realized she needed to spend more time with her then young daughter. She eventually found a home with a consulting group she had collaborated with while employed by the beverage company. She had spoken to their leadership team while they were doing consulting work at her then current employer. Once she decided to join their team, she was working on projects with her previous employer with someone she knew who knew her and her skills. The biggest benefit of that was that she could do great work, but it wasn't all-consuming and she didn't have to prove herself with a new team.

The big difference is that she works less than half the hours she worked before and makes about the same salary. The IT consultant has time with her family, at home and at her children's school. She shares about how much better her family's quality of life is. And she has time for passion projects, like helping people with their adoption journey.

Her advice for anyone interested in working part time:

• *Network.* Maintain relationships because you never know where those relationships will lead down the road.

• *Create a win-win scenario.* You want situations to be mutually beneficial. Know what your team and senior leadership need. Be aware of what you and your family need and ask for those things.

• *Don't make hasty decisions.* Take time in making decisions, both when looking at a transition and during the actual transition.

CHAPTER 4:

WHAT TO CONSIDER BEFORE YOU GO PART TIME

If moms are looking at long-term opportunities with a company so that they can feel supported and grow in the short- and long term, it's helpful to consider various aspects of a company and the industry culture before taking a specific path or starting a job. Do your homework on the company and industry. For example, look on the company or industry group websites or even at online companies that compile reviews from current and previous employees. Check out www.mompowerment.com for an updated list of companies that provide this type of information.

These resources help potential employees understand policies versus practice because they might be different. Look for articles and read the reviews from current and former employees or, better yet, speak to current and former employees about how policies and culture influence behavior as it relates to work-life balance. You can find alumni from your university or ask people in your own network for contacts at the company or in the industry. Start having those tough conversations, even before you are in an interview.

If you're already at a company, start talking to women in senior roles. Understand their path at the company. What, if anything, did they have to sacrifice to get to where they are? Look for any groups that help support women within the company. Find out about work-life balance initiatives or programs in place for when mothers come back from maternity leave. Talk to women in other groups because the path and support might vary from department to department or from one team to another. Understand everything your employer offers and start taking advantage of those programs.

Culture and Norms: Industry versus Company

When you're looking at current and future opportunities, take time to understand specific company and industry norms, which can dramatically impact work-life balance. Moms from all sorts of industries contributed to this book with their advice, insights, and stories. Some moms shared that their industry enabled moms to work part time with ease. Others mentioned that their part-time roles were hard to find. Some of the moms I interviewed talked about their companies having programs in place to enable moms to work part time, while others mentioned they were the first among hundreds to transition to a part-time schedule.

The culture and norms of an industry help enable or deter you from becoming a PPWM. And then sometimes it was a specific company's approach or policies that made a difference to the moms who shared their stories. The industry and company cultures work together to empower moms to work in roles with a reduced schedule or take away the power to make these changes in their schedule or role.

For example, I spoke with several moms who are social workers. One of these moms, who works about twenty-five hours per week in Michigan, explained that she gets support from her employer because the organization is dedicated to good relationships with parents. She described her employer as "a great place for her with a young child, because of the culture of the organization and the high level of flexibility." The organization specifically works with young children and their parents, and the company treats its employees the same way it does its clients.

Many of the moms I interviewed are in industries not necessarily known for their flexibility. One of these industries is healthcare. Several moms are medical providers, specifically either some sort of doctor or dentist. The two dentists, both in Austin, Texas, shared that more work-life balance was part of the reason for going into that side of the medical field. Before they even started graduate school, they knew they wanted to enter healthcare and specifically chose dentistry for the long-term opportunity for work-life balance versus going into a medical field with long hours.

The moms who work as doctors shared that the medical profession is not usually supportive of work-life balance. In fact, a few of the moms worked in academic roles within medicine to achieve the work-life balance they were looking for. A doctor in Austin, Texas, who works twenty-five to thirty hours per week, shared, "The working world is still pretty hostile to doctors working part-time." I spoke with an OB-GYN in Austin, Texas, who created a job share situation in a private practice. She and another doctor act as one doctor, with the same approach to patient care, each working part time. In this situation, part time is thirty to forty hours per week in comparison to full time, which is sixty or more hours per week.

That said, I spoke with moms in industries known for a lack of work-life balance such as finance, technology, and public accounting. I chatted with a chief financial officer (CFO) of a small hedge fund in the New York City area, who works twenty to twenty-five hours per week. She is an exception, but I mention her situation because, even in the most demanding industries and careers, you can still find or create professional part-time work opportunities. In the CFO's situation, she understood her value and the needs of the company, and could translate that into a part-time role. She mentioned she could work for a larger hedge fund, with even more responsibility and complexity to her role, but she likely wouldn't be able to work part time. Her current situation is a win-win for her and her employer.

The moms in technology and public accounting who shared their stories with me needed to create change in their lives. They had worked for several years for their employers and knew their own value. One mom who works for a large technology company needed to make a change because her kids were getting older and their activities were ramping up. She took a three-month sabbatical and then came back in a part-time role, focusing more on project-based work.

There are some companies willing to make major changes to keep high-performing employees at the company. One of these companies was in the petrochemical industry, which I wouldn't have initially considered as an industry or even company that focused on work-life balance. Part of the reason behind this flexibility was based on the moms being high performers. These companies didn't want to lose highly valuable team members who were willing to leave the workforce altogether if they couldn't find a reduced schedule and more work-life balance. And, it's not uncommon for these large petrochemical companies to have diversity initiatives in place to attract top talent, regardless of gender or race, and to figure out how to keep them at the company over the long-term.

There are companies and industries that don't have these types of policies in place. Of the moms I interviewed, almost 40 percent are entrepreneurs, many of whom started a company because they couldn't find the right work-life balance in the company where they worked or at other companies within their industry. I dedicate Chapter 8 to mom entrepreneurs because their needs are a bit different than those of PPWMs who are employed, whether at a small business or multinational corporation.

What to Look for in an Employer

For those moms who want to continue to work for a company and not go the entrepreneur route, I understand where you're coming from. My first year as a PPWM I was still at a large marketing firm where I had worked for about five and a half years full time before reducing my schedule.

If you're looking at your current employer or at other companies and you want to be at that company for the long-term, you want to make sure it's the right fit for your needs over time, right? Based on the interviews I did and on further research, there are six areas that seem to impact moms over the long term at a company, beyond specific job duties. Understanding these areas can help you find employers who are interested in the long-term growth of female employees and who understand that a woman's needs change over time.

Flexibility

One key concept is flexibility. If a company is interested in empowering employees to have work-life balance, it needs to provide employees with a level of flexibility. Perhaps your child is at home sick and you need to work from home for a day or two. Or maybe you have someone coming to your home to fix an appliance or install new equipment. What if you need to accompany your own mom to doctor appointments if her health is starting to deteriorate? Can you work from home or leave early? Is flexibility something the CEO talks about, but it's not actually used further down the ranks? You want an employer that not only has these policies and talks about them, but also empowers employees to use them. Each time shouldn't require a favor from your manager. You want managers to be supportive upfront and not engage human resources (HR) to take advantage of existing policy. (Keep in mind that HR might get involved to execute the plan you agree on with your manager.)

A makeup artist, who works ten to twenty-five hours a week in Austin, Texas, shared, "I feel I can say no to opportunities when they conflict with family obligations or family time." She can decline to work on a project or at an event and it won't impact her career. In her situation, part of the reason for flexibility is because her manager is also a mom. When you look for flexibility in a company, it's about empowering managers to allow for flexibility in dealing with their employees, as well as a level of flexibility that employees naturally have in any role. What happens if her manager changed? Would the company still provide that level of flexibility or was it an understanding manager who empowered employees?

If you're not sure which of these situations it is, ask around. Talk to other women who don't work for your same manager. Talk to employees in other departments and hear about their experiences and situations. Is it a series of one-off agreements or is it company policy?

Reduced Schedule Options or Openness to Options

Several moms who shared their story with me are engineers at a large multinational petrochemical company based in Houston, Texas. There are many moms with reduced schedules at the company. These employees are well-trained, have years of experience, and are high performing. In addition, the company has diversity initiatives and programs to keep women moving through different departments and up the ranks. These moms might have moved from one team or department to another when they wanted a reduced schedule, but the company was very open to reduced schedules. And, the company works with moms to figure out the right number of hours they individually need to work so that both employee and employer are happy with the situation.

A Connecticut-based mom in media sales shared that she gets support from her employer because the focus is on meeting goals, not on hours. She joined the company several years ago and works about twenty-five hours per week, which still allows her to achieve her sales goals.

What about in the situations where you are the first employee to work a part-time schedule? Even if no one has previously worked part time at the company, you want upper management and the company overall to be open to the possibility.

When a Chicago-based attorney, now working thirty hours per week, initially approached her employer about reducing her hours, the response was for her to "figure out what you need" and the company would support it. Her employer didn't want to lose her and was willing to be incredibly flexible to keep her from leaving, even though reduced schedules weren't commonly used at the firm where she works.

Work-life Balance Initiatives

Most companies, big or small, have some sort of benefits. The most basic is health benefits. What about work-life balance initiatives though? What other benefits does the company pay for, such as gym membership or backup childcare? For moms who have recently had a baby, how does the company support or facilitate pumping (e.g., provide a dedicated area for moms to pump, encourage pumping instead of treating it as an inconvenience, etc.)? What else does the company do to enable its employees to have more work-life balance?

What about work-life balance initiatives for those who aren't parents? Does the company give a paid (or even unpaid) sabbatical to employees, regardless of whether they are parents or not? Do employees actually use this benefit? What happens after they return from sabbatical? For most people I know, whose companies provide a sabbatical to employees after a certain number of years of service, they must stay for a specific amount of time after taking the sabbatical. If that's the case with your employer or the company you're considering, what happens after that time limit is up? If most employees leave, that might not be the best sign.

Let's be honest, it doesn't help to have work-life balance opportunities in place for show. So, how do they feel about you actually using those work-life balance tools and services? It's great to have initiatives in place, but it won't make a difference if it's frowned upon, should you choose to use them.

Career Growth for all Employees, both Full Time and Part Time

Most employees want to grow, whether they work full time or in a part-time capacity. Do companies seem to create a typical trajectory for women once they become mothers — the dreaded "mommy track?" Are there mothers working throughout the company at more senior levels? What has their career path looked like as full-time and especially as part-time employees?

How many women are there in senior leadership roles, regardless of if they are moms or not? What career paths have they followed? If they've had to claw their way to the top, fighting for every promotion, even though they were qualified, that might not be the best environment for supporting professional part-time roles for moms. And for that matter, look at the company's board. Are there women? Look at what types of initiatives they might be involved with. See if the company publicly talks about creating more opportunities for engaging women at more senior levels and see if that's actually happening.

What about those employees who are part time? If part-time employees' career growth is non-existent, companies could lose those engaged, productive employees. Or those employees who were engaged might become unmotivated workers who simply aren't giving their best. They will realize it won't matter if they're engaged. While career growth could be slower for a part-time employee, it doesn't have to be. What is the situation in the company where you work or would like to work?

Talk to moms who have transitioned to part time to understand their career growth. And take time to seek out those moms who transitioned to part time and back to full time to see how their careers adjusted to both situations. You want to understand the long-term impact of part time employment on their careers.

I've mentioned empowering employees and managers when it comes to decisions like schedules, but it's also important to keep part-time employees as empowered members of a team and not transition them to a mommy track situation. The part-time members of the team should be able to make decisions and take on important projects like any other member of the team. Isn't this how any engaged employee would like to be treated?

A media director who works twenty to twenty-five hours a week at a large marketing agency in Austin, Texas, transitioned to smaller pieces of business instead of the larger, more demanding clients when she moved into a part-time role. In addition, the company focused her more on East Coast clients instead of West Coast clients, which was more in line with her schedule needs. It would have been too hard to keep this marketing mom on large accounts with 24/7 demands. Her clients have changed, but she still has a meaningful role on smaller accounts with important needs.

A senior engineer who now works twenty hours at a large multinational petrochemical company in Houston, Texas, focuses on smaller projects, which are still critical pieces of overall projects. She is still at a high level of contribution, but on a smaller scale and that keeps her engaged and integral to her team.

Variety of Career Paths

How does a company look at career paths for PPWMs? Is there only one option for moms who want to work part time? Essentially, is it a take–it–or–leave–it approach? Have other part-time working moms moved into different areas and with a variety of opportunities to contribute?

An online media editor who works twenty to twenty-five hours per week, talked about how she wouldn't have grown professionally at her previously employer. She would have been in the "back seat," couldn't have taken on a bigger role, and would have worked more hours. In addition, the role would have been writing only, which would have limited her long-term career options. The difference with her current employer is that the culture allows for several career paths specifically designed for PPWMs. In addition, everyone works from home at her current employer. The woman who started the online publication worked for a major publication and then got pregnant, so she created an environment with a lot more work-life balance and flexibility for employees since it was what she also wanted.

Several of the engineers I spoke with at the multinational petrochemical company based out of Houston described a willingness from the company and from their managers to move the moms to other opportunities that made more sense for a part-time career approach. There are several options and positions to choose from. It depended on the mom's current skills, what skills she wanted to build, and what kind of work the mom wanted to do, in addition to the number of hours she wanted to work.

Maternity Policy

Although the focus of my book is on what happens after maternity leave, I want to take a moment to discuss maternity leave itself. From a business perspective, there are a few elements to keep in mind when an employee wants to have a baby. Look at all sides to really understand the company's maternity leave policy.

First, there is the legal side of things. The federal law that keeps companies from firing the women who take time off to have a baby is the Family and Medical Leave Act (FMLA). If you haven't yet had a child or dealt with major illness, you might not be familiar with FMLA. This is the law that requires employers to provide their employees with job protection and unpaid leave for up to twelve weeks once each 365 days for qualified family and medical reasons (e.g., having a baby or because of a major illness), whether yours or someone in your immediate family (e.g., your child, parent, spouse, etc.). You cannot lose your job unless the position is eliminated (e.g., no one will have the job because it no longer exists).

It's important to note that not all companies must comply with federal FMLA requirements. Companies with fifty or more employees within a seventy-five-mile radius of the office must comply with this law. And if you work for the local, state, or federal government or a public or private school, you are eligible for FMLA as long as you've been with the organization for at least twelve months. Those twelve months don't have to be a consecutive, but they must have happened within the past seven years. And, an added requirement is that employees must work at least 1,250 hours during those twelve months. Essentially, some part-time employees might not be eligible. When you break it down, employees who have worked at least twenty-four hours per week over those twelve months are eligible.

Even with recent hires, some companies still choose to follow FMLA guidelines. Some small businesses don't have to follow the FMLA guidelines, but they do it anyway because work-life balance matters to them. And, let's be honest, it's a great way to attract top talent who might have been interested in working for a larger company.

Second, there is the issue of paid or unpaid maternity leave. At the time this book was written, maternity leave policy in the business world in the United States and at the government level was getting more attention, but the overall approach in the United States is not even in the same league as other developed nations. The United States is the only developed nation in the world that doesn't provide paid maternity leave at a national level. As a point of comparison, most other developed nations provide anywhere from six months to more than a year of maternity leave that is paid at full or partial salary. In fact, according to an analysis of the top sixty employers done by a nonprofit that advocates for paid family leave, the Paid Leave for the United States (PL+US), and Global Health Vision, "the majority of the top employers in the U.S. offer no paid family leave or are not transparent about their paid family leave policy."[1]

Why does it matter if it's paid or not? Imagine not receiving a salary for four, six, or sixteen weeks while you're taking care of a new member of your family. Most families can't take unpaid maternity leave for an extended time because of the financial implications. They can't afford it.

Another interesting element is that a company might not pay salary in the normal way during maternity leave. In my situation, my maternity leave was paid through short-term disability and I received eight weeks instead of the usual six because I had a Caesarian section (C-section). I took an additional four weeks that was a combination of sick time and vacation days to have a total of twelve weeks of paid maternity. That basically wiped out my vacation for the rest of the year. The challenge is that when it comes to short-term disability and other ways to pay out maternity leave, it's inconsistent since policies can vary from state to state.

You might be wondering why maternity leave matters. Companies are starting to recognize the need for paid time off after having a baby. Giving birth isn't usually easy work and don't forget that a C-section is major surgery. Maternity leave helps moms allow their bodies to heal, form a stronger bond with baby, and even get babies into a rhythm, which is hard to do when baby is a month old. These are integral to helping moms get back to work, able to focus, and be at peak productivity during work hours after maternity leave.

And, finally, there is the issue of how work will happen when a mother is out on maternity leave, which could be weeks or months. Does your work stop for the time you're gone, so that you come back to what seems like a mountain of work and you're forever catching up? Is the work divided among your team or colleagues, so that your role is covered through others? Maybe they hire someone temporarily while you're out on maternity leave. Does the approach vary from manager to manager or by department? Ask around to see what happens because this might provide some interesting insights into how they value their female team members and how they help reintegrate them back into work once they return from maternity leave.

Some companies provide part-time opportunities as moms get back from maternity leave with limited, if any, travel, in addition to services specifically for these moms, so that their needs are fully supported and their reentry is gradual. More companies are starting to offer this reentry approach as moms come back from maternity leave in efforts to keep moms from leaving the workforce.[3] Especially in highly competitive industries where companies invest heavily in their employees, companies want to ensure moms return after maternity leave.[3]

The general and specific information on maternity leave can be complicated and difficult to understand, so make sure to do some digging using all sorts of resources, including conversations with moms at the company. You might be able to find moms to talk to through the alumni base at your school or through your own network. And consider the maternity policy and how current moms use that policy. Does the website or employee manual say twelve weeks, but no one takes more than six? Look on www.mompowerment.com for links to resources that have more information on maternity policies.

Fair Pay for Part-time Work

When you hear the term "fair pay," it's usually associated with how women are paid versus men. According to the nonprofit Institute for Women's Policy Research (IWPR), in 2016 a woman earned about $0.82 for every dollar a man earns.[4] The IWPR describes itself as a "501(c)(3) tax exempt organization that conducts and communicates research to inspire public dialogue, shape policy, and improve the lives and opportunities of women of diverse backgrounds, circumstances, and experiences."

When I refer to fair pay for part-time work, I mean that part-time employees are paid based on value and not the reduction of hours. About 10 percent of the moms I interviewed make a six-figure salary for working twenty to forty hours (remember, that compares to sixty or more hours in some industries or companies). The salaries for this 10 percent of interviewees were based on their contribution to the company and their productivity, not only the hours they work.

That is the ideal type of scenario – companies looking at contribution and productivity – instead of looking at hours alone. The companies where these moms work are looking at the value of an employee instead of a comparison of full-time versus part-time hours alone. You want a company that doesn't necessarily do a simple formula of dropping your salary 25 percent because you drop your hours to thirty from forty, especially if you're saying you will do your full-time job in less time. You shouldn't be penalized for cutting back hours if you're able to continue to do your job more efficiently. Shouldn't there be a reward for being more productive?

In summary:

There are many aspects of a job and industry that can impact your decision to transition to a part-time role:

- Consider the cultural norms in the industry and at the employer to understand policies versus how they are implemented.
- Understand what kinds of flexibility companies provide to employees and what work-life balance initiatives are in place.
- Take time to look at career path opportunities and overall growth opportunities that exist for full-time employees.

- Consider part-time career opportunities and the general openness to a part-time career model, even if the positions don't currently exist.
- Understand how part-time employees are compensated.
- Look into maternity policy at the company.

CHAPTER 5:

UNDERSTAND YOUR MOTIVATION FOR CHANGE

Now that we understand some of the considerations before you even think about going part time, let's move on to your why. About 20 percent of the moms talked about some aspect of figuring out the motivation behind wanting a change in their career approach.

As you go through this section, you might find it helpful to talk through it with someone. Reach out to a trusted colleague at work who might be in the same situation. Ask your significant other to talk through it with you. Consider talking to a friend, sibling, parent, etc. Or it might be beneficial to reach out to a trusted career advisor. This can be the foundation to next steps, so talk to whomever can help you better understand your feelings about your work situation.

First, figure out your motivation. Discussing the reasons why you want to go part time should happen before taking other steps, since this motivation becomes your guide. Essentially, it's why you're looking at changing your approach to career in the first place. This motivation will help you understand what aspects of a part-time role you need to consider, look for, analyze, request, or even negotiate. You want to make sure you're getting out of this new scenario what you're looking for. Or maybe what you're looking for will take you down the path of entrepreneurship or into a career pivot if your why tells you that you're no longer fulfilled in what you've been doing. And, once you understand this, you'll understand what is motivating you and what you want your time to look like in a part-time role.

For example, if wanting to spend more time with your child is the driving force behind making a change, then look for a job that allows you to work while your kids are in school, so that it doesn't cut into your family time.

Or maybe you want time to spend time with an aging, sick parent. Are there appointments that you'd like to be present for? Will that require a job with more flexibility and not necessarily fewer hours or will it require less office time *and* fewer hours?

Second, think through whether a part-time approach to your career is the best path to helping you achieve your motivation. As much as I believe in part time as an amazing option for moms, I understand that this isn't the right fit for all moms. Understand if part-time is a better fit than a job change to a less demanding role or company. Or maybe you're really looking for a role with flexible hours altogether. Or your motivation might lead you to a work–from-home situation as a better fit with your needs. If you don't understand your motivation, how do you know which scenario meets those needs? If you're not sure why you want it, how will you know if a change will even help?

Third, understanding your motivation helps you with matching your role and activities to your why. If you're interested in working part time so you can volunteer at your child's school, you probably don't want a job where you travel away from your family for consecutive days every week, even if you work fewer than forty hours a week. You either need a role that enables flexibility during work hours, allows you to start after the school day starts, or ends before your child's school day is over, so that you can find time to volunteer at the school.

And finally, when you've thought through your motivation, you're better able to sell the idea to your manager or senior management. When speaking to decision-makers at the company where you work, you will be able to articulate what you're asking for and what you're willing to negotiate. It's helpful to brainstorm a bit by yourself or even with a friend who understands your work and family circumstances. You want to think through your motivation and the elements you're negotiating so that they match. You also can think through trade-offs for work and home. Ultimately, you're trying to design win-win scenarios with your employer, so figure out what "winning" looks like for you and imagine how it looks for your company. (Check out Chapter 12 for more information on this.)

Maybe what you figure out as you look at your motivation is that this is the time to pivot into a new career or to start your own business. If you don't take the time to understand your why, you won't know that you need to make bigger changes instead of asking for a reduction in your hours.

One of the main considerations you need to understand is how this decision to change your approach to your career will impact your financials. I've dedicated a whole chapter to that topic, since it's important with short-term and long-term implications (see Chapter 7 for more).

How to Figure Out your Motivation

Working part time allows me to have more flexibility and more consistent and deeper engagement with my two boys. I figured out long before having kids that part time would eventually be part of my approach to my career. I worked at marketing agencies for about five years before returning to school for an MBA. Not everyone realizes it, but working at a marketing agency can be very demanding. On a good week, I worked fifty-five hours.

After working at various marketing agencies for more than five years, I wanted my life back. I decided to take things into my own hands and went to graduate school for my MBA. I worked long hours before grad school and I didn't see a way to change that without making a shift in my career.

Fast forward almost seven years after grad school when my husband and I started our family. Rather unexpectedly, my timeline for working part time moved up. It was a long-term goal, but I started working part time as I returned from maternity leave. I have worked part time since becoming a mom in 2011. At first, I worked part time for a large company, where I had worked for five and a half years full time in various roles. And after about a year, I focused only on my strategic marketing consulting business, which I had done as a side hustle for more than seven years at that point.

The benefit to me to work part time is that I am the face my boys see at the end of their day. I want them to know I am always there for them, to celebrate something they're proud of and provide support on not-so-great days. That interaction with my boys is important to me.

I volunteer and attend events at their schools. I'm able to be engaged with other parents in their school communities and that connection is important to me. I could stay home full time and do the same, but I'm not interested in that approach. I like using my expertise and experience to help companies with their strategic marketing challenges. And I like having my own goals and achievements outside of motherhood. It helps with my own personal identity and keeps me satisfied in all areas of my life.

You might be reading this and say "I want more of that" or "I need a change" and yet not be able to articulate the motivation behind it. You now know it's important to understand your "why," but how do you uncover it in your own situation?

Figuring out your motivation takes some soul searching and self-reflection. The questions I'm including will help you figure out your own motivation for wanting to change your career approach and maybe even lead you to ask your own questions that uncover even more behind your motivation.

Ask "Why?"

It's helpful to ask, "Why do I want this change?" That might sound simple, but there is a bit more to it. You know your motivation (e.g., spending time with your kids), but what is the "why" behind that? Drill down a bit more to understand the underlying motivation and not what is at the surface. Ask "why" a few times to start figuring out the real answer behind your motivation. You might be surprised at what you uncover.

What Do You Want to Change?

Now that you're starting to understand why you want to make changes, what is it that you want to change? Try to be specific. Don't simply say, "I want more work-life balance." Understanding the "what" will help you make adjustments, big or small, that align with what you want to change.

For example, do you want to start later or end earlier so you can drop off and/or pick up your child? Do you want fewer days in the office, so that you can spend one or several whole days with your child? I wanted a combination of both, so my hours were capped at twenty per week, which I split over three work days per week.

What does it Look Like?

It's helpful to do some brainstorming on what these changes look like in the best case. If it helps, visualize what you want and try to describe the scene or picture in your mind. That might help you think through and put words to what you want. Think about the elements that you want to include and consider what must be included (i.e., your non-negotiables). What benefit will you get out of working part time? Now that you understand what it looks like, you can use that visual as part of your plan when you speak with your manager or senior leadership, or if you start looking at entrepreneurship as a better way to achieve what you're looking for.

On the professional side, analyze your accomplishments. When you look at those, dive into what you most enjoyed about the role, project, or situation. This approach can help as a starting point for conversation with a manager on what you wish to concentrate on going forward.

Consider the personal side. In my case, I knew that I wanted to do some activities with our newborn, such as mommy and me music class. What did my schedule need to be to make that happen? In addition, if I wanted to volunteer at my son's school, what would my schedule need to be to make that happen?

How can you combine what you want professionally and personally so that it gets you what you want? Take time to see how these two aspects come together.

Your Feelings About Work

As you look at your "why" and "what," take a bit of time to understand how you are feeling about work. Do you have a new manager who you're not very excited about? Maybe you're angry or frustrated about things that have recently changed. Are you disappointed with your bonus? Perhaps policies at work have changed and become less flexible. Have you taken on a new project that you're less than excited about, even though you expressed concerns about its impact on your work-life balance?

There are so many aspects to how you feel about work and what drives those feelings. Think through how you're feeling. And ask the different levels of "why" here as well.

Time for Career Change versus Change in Career Approach

Are you still excited about your career? You might not be excited about your job, but are you still excited about what you generally do? You know you want a change, but you enjoy what you do. This is a sign that you might need a change in your career approach and not a change in career or industry.

Are you still happy with the company you work for? If the answer is yes, but you're still feeling hesitant, maybe you need to see what is available on other teams or in other departments. Talk to people about their experience with a different manager, on another team, or in a department outside of your own.

If the answer is no when you start thinking through how excited you are about the company you work for, perhaps it's time to look at other companies and leave your current employer. Consider if there are other companies in the same industry or even related industries that provide more of what you're looking for. Understanding your motivation will help you figure out which companies are a good fit and which ones to avoid.

If you're unhappy with your company or industry overall, is part of what's driving your motivation a desire to become an entrepreneur instead of working for someone else? Is it time to manage your own business? Don't take this leap lightly. Being an entrepreneur is not easy, but it does put you in the driver's seat on your hours, growth, and even types of projects and clients. Is this the change you're looking for?

For almost 40 percent of moms I interviewed this was the case. They couldn't find what they were looking for at a company, so they started their own business. They control when they work, how many hours, who they work with (this becomes even more the case as they became more seasoned entrepreneurs), and even which days they work. Most agree that it's not easy though. It takes a lot of work. (More on that in Chapter 8.)

Has the time come for a career overhaul? If you're unhappy with your career, could this be an opportunity to pivot or to make a clear break to do something different. Maybe it's not a transition to part time that you need; maybe you need to transition into a new career. As I mentioned, a few of the moms who shared their story transitioned to part time as a way to do additional training to start a different career altogether.

I spoke with a mom in San Antonio, Texas, who had worked in marketing for several years after getting an MBA from a top program. Soon after her older son was born, she decided to be a SAHM. When she went back to work years later, she was in an operations role, working twenty hours per week as a director of operations for a consulting firm. She had already worked in her original area of expertise and she was more interested in the right role instead of a role in her area of study.

A Long Island based-mom, who works about twenty hours a week for a construction business, is starting to explore more of her interest in creating systems and infrastructure for businesses. She created a few systems at work and continues to expand her knowledge in this area of interest.

Will More Time in Your Day Make a Difference?

Will having more time make a difference in your day? Maybe you have enough time in your day already to get everything done. It's not that you need more time, you need more *flexible* time. Or do you need both?

Understanding this can help you decide if you a part-time role might work better than a flexible schedule. If you're looking for more flexible time, maybe you need to transition to a flexible schedule. Or maybe working from home is what will give you more flexibility in your day. Essentially, you can pinpoint what type of schedule is ideal for your needs.

As a bonus, understanding the answers to these questions can help you understand how to structure your time and the days you work.

And it gives you specific ideas of how to negotiate with your current or new manager, senior leaders, or even clients if you go the entrepreneurial route.

Recent Versus Long-term Interest

Figure out when you started thinking about needing a change. Is this interest in a new career approach a long-term goal? Is it something you only recently started thinking about? Did something recently happen at home or at work that got you thinking differently? Have you recently changed managers and you're seeing that your new manager isn't as flexible? Are you recently pregnant and thinking through your situation post-maternity leave? All of these questions about timing help you understand if you're reacting to something recent or if it's been a long time coming and that might impact how you look at your options now and in the future.

Temporary or Long-term Transition?

Do you want to do this for a few years while your kids are younger or is this how you want to permanently approach your career moving forward? Many of the moms who wanted more time with their children started working part time as a temporary situation, which they expected would last a few years. After experiencing life working part time, it became more long-term or even permanent for them. Of the more than 110 moms I interviewed, 39 percent shared they will not or are not likely to head back to work full time. About 25 percent said they will go or are likely to head back to work full time, although for some moms, that is more than a decade away. And about 37 percent were undecided with an answer of "maybe."

Findings on Motivation from the 110 Interviews

A primary motivation for the moms going to a part-time approach to their career was to spend more time with family. For some moms, they *wanted* this. For others, they *needed* to make the shift. For those moms who needed to make a change, it was often to help a family member overcome some sort of challenge. In some situations, the challenges were a child's developmental delays or major changes in behavior that needed to be addressed quickly. Other moms needed to care for a sick family member. Several moms needed to lower their own stress levels, which were affecting their health. A few moms shared that they were on the verge of divorce because it was all too much. All of these moms looked to working part time to help overcome the challenge they faced.

One of the circumstances that most surprised me about transitioning to a professional part-time role was to home school their children. Less than a handful of moms I spoke with do this, but I'm always surprised and impressed by this concept, especially when it's a mom who works (part time or full time). I'm sharing this because this might be one of the reasons why you're considering transitioning to this approach. According to this handful of moms, it's doable to home school your kids and work.

In summary:

Understanding your motivation is a key element to starting the process of transitioning to a part-time career approach.

- You want to understand why you're interested in this potential transition as well as what you want to change.
- Think through what's happening at the office and if that's impacting your overall feeling about work and driving you to want change.
- Consider if career change (e.g., role, department, industry) is a better option than a change in career model.
- Look at other options to see if they're a better fit, such as work–from-home, flexible schedule, and even entrepreneurship.

CHAPTER 6:

UNDERSTANDING IMPLICATIONS OF BECOMING PPWM

Now that you understand your motivation for wanting to work part time in your career, the next step is starting to think through how it will impact you and your family. The transition will likely affect your life, professionally and personally. Make sure that those changes are acceptable to you and your family from a personal perspective, and your team and manager on the professional side. You asked tough questions on why you want to make this change. Now it's time to ask the tough questions about how the transition will happen. Think through the short-term and long-term impact and what adjustments you must make, now that you know why you want to make the transition to a professional part-time role.

Career Implications

One of the questions I hear from moms interested in transitioning to a part-time approach to their career is "Will this transition hurt me professionally?" I can't answer that. The impact on your career is unique to your situation and you probably know that better than I ever could. I am sharing questions that help you think through the transition, so that you can better understand how it will affect your career. Once you understand that, you can decide if those effects are acceptable to you, your family, your team, your manager, etc.

So, how are you going to think through the implications on your career? These questions will help get you started:

High Performers

Are you considered a high performing and valuable employee to your manager and/or your employer? Will the transition to part-time work make you less of a high performer in the eyes of your manager or senior management? Take time and really think through these initial questions.

Many of the moms I interviewed shared they were and still are high performers. They weren't hurt by making the transition to a part-time role. In fact, the companies they worked for were often flexible and open to enabling more work-life balance, so that these high performers wouldn't leave. Is that the case for you or are high performers traditionally full-time employees who will put in extra hours as necessary? What happens to other high performers who have asked for changes in career approach?

Will not being available 24/7 have a negative impact on your career? Will you lose clout in your company or industry and no longer be considered an integral member of the team if you shift gears? If so, the question becomes whether that matters to you or not. Are you comfortable with being a high performer who goes against the norm, if there is one? A social work supervisor in Michigan, who works twenty hours per week, shared, "I have to deal with not being a go-to person all the time. Letting go was the biggest challenge I had to deal with." The part-time social work supervisor added that "In my full-time role, I felt the world would fall apart if I wasn't there at work, but it's all OK when I'm not there."

Career Stage

At what stage is your career? Some of the moms who are entrepreneurs designed their business from the beginning with work-life balance or even work-life integration in mind. Most people cannot do this if they work for an employer or sometimes even if they work for themselves. If you're at a more junior level, is this the right time to try to make this request or will you have more negotiating power at a more senior level? If you realize that you could have more negotiating power later (which is likely the case), can you wait a few years? If so, how long?

Relationship with your Employer and Manager

Consider how you feel toward your manager and your company. Or is it time for a change at your employer? If you enjoy what you do, but don't like your manager or don't think he or she will support your change in career approach, maybe another team with more flexibility is a better option. If you like what you do, but you're not as excited about your employer, it could be time to look at switching to another company or even starting your own business. It's when you realize you don't like what you do any more, that you should start to think about major change, such as career pivot. If you start considering change in your career, take a step back and understand if you're running away from something or toward something. Running away from something might not get you to a better place professionally.

Short-term Versus Long-term

Is shifting to a part-time career approach a short-term or long-term option? Does one or the other work better for you or are they equal? Why? Will you be in a part-time role for a few years or is this something you plan on integrating into your life permanently until you retire? Do you think one option will be better for your career (and your family)? Why do you think that is the case?

Potential Missed Opportunities

Those moms I interviewed who do want to continue to move up

the ranks seem to look at the part-time approach as a temporary situation. After a few years, those moms are planning to go back full time (or they already have since their interviews). Since the moms interested in going back full time at some point have stayed in the workforce by going part time, they won't generally deal with the hurdles of reentering the workforce after extended time away.

If you transition to a part-time role and miss an opportunity for career growth or promotion, how will that affect your own perspective on your career and family? Some of the moms I spoke with shared that they missed opportunities for promotion, but they were OK with that.

Is this a moment when your career is taking off? Is this your moment at work or is this a moment of learning and growing without a focus on promotion, during which you can lean out a bit? What lateral moves, instead of moving up the corporate ladder, might better position you down the road? For some moms who shared their stories, their careers have shifted a bit and they're not as interested in running a large department or moving to the most senior leadership levels of a company as they once were. They would like to move up a level or two more and learn new skills along the way, maintaining a focus on work-life balance. They don't want to get promotions that take them to the point of burning out and/or seeing their families for a few hours each week. Their interest is now steady, consistent growth over time so that they have more work-life balance in place long-term.

Personal Implications

Another question I hear is "What changes will I have to make at home when I start working part time?" When moms shift from one career approach to another, there is usually an implication for you and/or your family. Not sure how to look at those implications or even how to figure them out? These questions might help you figure out this side of the equation.

Time Implications

Is this a season when your family needs more of your time and attention? Is it that you need more time to have a positive effect on the situation or do you simply need more flexibility in your schedule and not more time? Or maybe it's both. There is a difference and it changes what you ask for of your current employer or what changes you need to make in your schedule.

What will you do with more time available to spend time with family or on personal interests? What you will do with your time might already be addressed when you figure out your motivation, but it's important to explore that topic if you haven't yet. Understand what your day will look like and how you will use the new time you have, whether it's spending more time with family, learning new skills, helping with an aging family member, or whatever else you'd like to fill that time with. Map out what you want the additional time in your schedule to include, which also helps you figure out how much you really need to reduce your schedule.

Conversation with your Significant Other

Have you spoken to your significant other about your interest in transitioning to a part-time role? If yes, what did you cover? How did the conversation go? If no, what are you planning on including in the conversation? Countless moms shared in interviews that it's important to get input and support from your significant other when you're looking at changing your career model. The conversation can be hard and happen over time instead of trying to cover everything in one chunk of time. And structuring the conversation will depend on your communication style as an individual and as a couple. If you are wondering what types of things to include in your conversation, these questions might help:

What are your thoughts about the financial side of things? (I have a whole chapter devoted to finances, so check out Chapter 7 for more information.)

- What types of changes will happen in your household?
- What are the types of changes you are expecting related to the different duties for both parents?
- What kind of support do you want and need from your significant other?
- What type of help are you looking at from outside the home?
- What are your thoughts on expectations from both you and your significant other? What are your partner's expectations?
- Are there elements that might be related to your significant other's job (e.g., medical benefits)?
- What ground rules should there be on what happens when a child is sick or sent home from school?

See the template on www.mompowerment.com to help you prepare before and take notes during the conversation(s) with your significant other.

Personal Support Structure

What changes will you need to make in your personal support structure (e.g., sitter or housekeeper)? (I'll talk a bit more about this in Chapter 18.) More than 10 percent of the moms suggested getting help as a key piece of advice. That help might be a babysitter or nanny or sending your children to mothers' day out or daycare for part of the day. It might also be help from the business side, whether paying for a tool or help via a specialist or virtual assistant. Figure out what your support structure currently is and how you need it to change when you transition to a part-time role. Have those changes in place or understand their timing before you transition so that you have time to adjust.

If you work from home, and if you have young children who aren't yet in school, you will likely still need someone to watch them. That could be a nanny, babysitter, or even daycare or mothers' day out.

If care outside of the home isn't an option for whatever reason, consider switching off days with another mom, so that both of you have time to do work without interruption. Be creative in how you find non-traditional care options like this. You will need time to get work done.

Figuring out the right schedule might help with this aspect. For example, if you have kids in school, it might be better to work five days per week in the morning until pick up time. If you're paying for daycare and pay for the day, maybe you want more full days. It will likely be cheaper and it gives you big blocks of time to focus on work.

Impact of a New Schedule on Family Life

How will your new schedule impact your family? Your new schedule may require you to think differently about your family's needs. For example, if you work three eight-hour days as your schedule transitions to twenty-four hours per week instead of the usual forty, does that mean you need different childcare than when you worked forty hours? If you have had full-time help and you no longer need it, will that person work for you part time?

For most moms I spoke with, there was a positive impact on their families with several benefits when they went to a part-time approach to their careers. For example, maybe your kids can now start getting involved with an activity that you avoided because it required too much coordination when you worked full time. If so, how can you balance getting your child involved in those activities without it infringing on whatever you're hoping to get out of a reduced schedule?

Consider Your Feelings

What are your feeling as it relates to these changes? While you hope these changes will have a positive effect on your short-term and long-term situation, they can also be overwhelming, especially initially. Understand how you're feeling about these potential changes and what is driving any anxiety or coming up as areas of concern.

Consider scaling back on the proposed changes or making a transition plan to avoid switching from one approach to another as you flip on a light switch. For many moms, these changes don't happen overnight. You might need time to adjust to changes at home. You can make the transition happen as quickly or as slowly as you need to, once you understand what needs to be done and how any changes might affect you and your family.

If you're not sure how you're feeling or how to work out your feelings, reach out to friends and family or even a professional to help you talk it out, and ask and address the tough questions. And don't hesitate to contact a career or life coach who specializes in career or life transitions to better understand the career and personal implications. Have him or her walk you through what that looks like in your situation with your career and family.

Impact on Personal Growth Goals

I set personal growth goals for myself over periods of time. I am goal oriented and need to be working toward something or I get frustrated and might even lose momentum. Some are small, especially as I break down larger goals into bite-sized pieces, and some are for the year, so they are bigger.

If you set your overall career and personal goals or developed a personal plan, how will a transition to part time impact those goals or that plan? Are the changes acceptable to you? For the moms who are high performers, you might already have an overall growth plan, whether done with your manager or as you set your own growth goals. When you look at your overall goals and plan, how does working part time fit in?

For example, if you want to be promoted to partner in three years and you are two levels away, is that a likely goal once you transition to a part-time role? It still could be or it might not. Or it might be something you need to negotiate as you move into a part-time role. You can reasonably figure out whether or not you can hit your goals with a change in your career approach. And only you know what areas are important enough that you need to have those topics as part of your conversation with your manager or senior leadership from the professional side and with your significant other and family on the personal side. Only you know what's in your personal plan, if you have one, and what changes might happen if you change your career approach.

Trade-Offs

What trade-offs, if any, are you considering? Are those trade-offs acceptable to you? Why or why not? When it comes to working part time as your career approach, chances are you will be making trade-offs, whether in your career, on the personal side, or both. Consider how trade-offs impact not only you but also your family and your team. What are you willing to give up to change to a part-time approach? Or, can you have all the pieces you're looking for personally and professionally, even with a part-time approach? If you've already started thinking through your motivation, you can better understand which trade-offs are acceptable and which ones are non-negotiable.

These questions will start you down the path to understand if this transition is the right career approach for you and you will see what areas you might want to further explore. You can also start to get a better understanding as to whether this is the right time and, if not, when would be a better time. The questions also help you get started on developing a plan for yourself and your family and for your team and manager.

In summary:

You want to understand the personal and professional implications of transitioning to a professional part-time role.

- How will a transition to fewer hours impact your performance and position within company and industry?
- Consider career stage and personal growth goals.
- Have a conversation with your significant other if you haven't already.
- Understand what trade-offs you're willing to make or not make (non-negotiables).
- Consider implications on family life and what support structure you will need to put in place.
- Do a check-in to see how you're feeling and reacting to this potential change in career approach.

CHAPTER 7:

LOOKING AT THE FINANCIAL SIDE OF BECOMING A PPWM

I'VE MENTIONED THE FINANCIAL side of things several times because this topic came up a lot in the stories that moms shared – in almost 10 percent of the interviews. And financials were sometimes a negative or a challenge when moms work part time. And, it wasn't only about salary. With all the advice and insights moms shared on this topic, I thought it fitting that it have its own chapter with short-term and long-term considerations.

Financial Stability

Several moms I interviewed talked about the need to be "financially stable" and "get your financial house in order." For a few of these moms, it was because they wanted to be able to walk away from their jobs to become SAHMs if things didn't work out. Let's be honest, could you walk away from your job if your manager or senior leadership said no to your request to work part time? What would happen financially if you left your part-time professional role if it didn't meet your expectations? Those were the types of questions some of the moms had before making sure they were financially ready. And for others, they were transitioning to an entrepreneurial endeavor, not only to a professional part-time role, so they wanted to be financially ready to start building their businesses.

Living within your Means

A few moms explained that financial stability stemmed from wanting to make few, if any, changes in their lifestyle. The concept of living within your means came up in some of these conversations. That way moms had choices and didn't have to worry as much about the financial impact of transitioning to a part-time role. A certified financial consultant in the Austin, Texas area, who works about thirty-five hours a week, talked about keeping overall costs low and adding services as your salary goes up. For example, instead of buying a bigger, more expensive house when you start making more money (assuming your current location and living situation are fine), you want to get more services such as housekeeping or a babysitter for a date night each week. Her suggestions stemmed from a desire to live better instead of bigger as you move through the ranks or your business grows.

The Question of Value versus Hours

Many moms who read this book will assume that they should analyze their finances with the assumption that they will get a pay cut if they cut their hours. And most of the questions here help you think through the impact of a pay cut.

Ideally though, not everyone who reduces her hours will get a pay cut, or at least not to the same level of the cut in hours. This is where you need to understand your value as an employee.

For example, you're asking for a reduction of ten hours, so that you work thirty instead of the usual forty. (And, let's keep in mind that few professionals only work forty hours in a full-time role.) Seems straightforward, but that's not always the case. What if you cut your time to thirty, but you will continue to manage your full workload?

In that situation, should you get a pay cut when you're producing the same level of work, even if you're cutting your hours by 25 percent?

What if you're a highly productive and efficient employee and you produce more than your colleagues on most days. Again, if you're cutting your hours to twenty, your salary will likely drop. But should your salary be cut in half? If you're a high performer and continue with your same work ethic, won't you continue to produce more on an hourly basis?

If you're going to reduce your schedule by half, your salary will drop, but the question is by how much? When you're highly efficient and productive, your salary shouldn't be cut in half. So, how do you get around this? Take the financials out of the initial conversation with your manager or senior leadership. Your perspective and subsequent negotiation is about productivity and contribution to your team and company at that point, not about money.

This is where you need to think through your value and not only your request for a cut in hours. If you've already considered your accomplishments as it relates to the request to reduce your hours, this should be relatively easy. What would have happened without you working on the projects you've been a part of? You have the results of your efforts. This can go a long way to show your value and how integral you are to the team.

Then think through what your employer would have to do to replace you. There would be cost to find a new person and then train and get him or her up to speed. That might change your thoughts on the financial perspective and how you adjust your negotiation strategy. And you can help create a win-win with all these factors in mind. (We cover more about this in Chapter 11 on the business perspective.)

Value might also impact your pricing as an entrepreneur. One mom who has her own entertainment and food business in Austin, Texas, mentioned that she had to understand the total value of her time, not only time she is physically with a client. In her case, she estimates time to get to and back from a venue as part of her overall fee since it's time out of her day. This additional time is built into her pricing.

Your Per Hour Rate Might Go Up

Your per hour rate might not go down; it might actually go up. Even if you are staying at your current employer, your hourly rate still might go up, depending on how you negotiate your final adjusted salary. As I mentioned, you can change the focus to productivity and contribution, so that the financial part becomes easier to negotiate.

If you're a seasoned employee or have highly sought-after skills, you might be able to charge a premium hourly rate if you go out on your own. A counselor who owns her own business in Lancaster, Pennsylvania, shared, "It's doable to work less and make equal income."

Keep in mind that if you're starting a business, it might take time to get back up to your current salary. Some moms I spoke with had an easy time getting to their current salary and, for others, it took time, even as seasoned professionals with years of experience. Prepare for the slow, steady approach for building business and, if your business grows quickly, it's a bonus to you financially speaking.

Financial Questions

Let's start thinking through the financial side of things. It's not uncommon to get a pay cut, especially if you don't negotiate based on your value. If you're thinking through transitioning to a part-time role for the first time, you might not know what to think through from a financial perspective. The questions I'm including are from the perspective of someone who is likely going to have a reduction in income. These aren't the only questions to consider, but they definitely get you started on understanding the financial implications, both short-term and long-term. We're ultimately trying to figure out if you and your family can afford for you to transition to a part-time role, *if* you were to get a pay cut. If you don't expect a pay cut to be part of the equation, you still might be able to use some of these questions. And starting to ask these questions might help you understand how much you need to make to maintain your standard of living with or without limited changes.

Drop in Income Level

Some moms will receive a pay cut as they reduce their hours. How will you deal with that decrease in income? I don't have the answer, but I do have questions to get you started on understanding the implication of a pay cut.

- What changes, if any, will you and your family need to make if your income level falls, however small?
- Will you need to make changes in the types of activities your children are involved in?
- Are there any services that you might need to rethink (e.g., housekeeper)? Hint: This might seem like an easy line item to remove, but read Chapter 18 before making that change. For example, instead of removing these services altogether, consider reducing the service. You could have a cleaning service come every other week instead of each week or once a month.
- What level of income do you need, even as a part-time employee? Hint: Figure out what monthly expenses you need to cover, including things like retirement or 529 savings. Keep in mind that some of your costs, like childcare, might go down, so make those adjustments in your budget as well.
- How much do you need to make to not have any lifestyle changes?
- Can you create a passive income stream to continue to have a higher level of income now, which will continue even when your income gets back to its current level?

Retirement

When you decide to transition to a part-time role, it's not only the short-term potential decrease in income that you need to consider. Even if your income doesn't go down, there can be long-term implications, including retirement. Start thinking through the impact on retirement to help you understand if this change in your career approach is right for your situation. Especially as an entrepreneur, there is upside to doing well when it comes to retirement. Talk to your HR department or a financial planner to understand further implications as they relate to retirement.

- If you work for a company and you transition to a part-time role, how will it affect your employer matching your 401K?
- Are you fully vested in your 401K plan? If not, how much longer will it be until that happens?
- Are you planning on retiring soon?
- Does your retirement plan require your current income?
- Is your overall retirement plan flexible?
- How close are you to your retirement goals?
- Can you make up any lost income in a few years? Hint: This might require you going back to work full time in the near or distant future, so factor your thoughts on that element here.
- Can you create something that allows for passive income to make up the difference in retirement funds you might be currently missing out on?
- How will working part time affect your social security?

Other Financial Considerations

There are several other areas to consider, especially benefits, taxes, and the long-term impact of financial planning that make up your financial health. If you're wondering why benefits is included in a chapter about financials, benefits often make up a large part of compensation in the United States. According to the most recent U.S. Bureau of

Labor Statistics update, benefits make up 30 to 37 percent of an employee's compensation, depending on the type of employer.[1] Again, talk to HR or a tax or financial planner to understand your specific situation.

- If you have insurance through your employer, how will going to part time affect your medical and dental insurance (and any other benefits)?

- Is there a minimum number of hours at which you maintain your benefits? If you need or want more coverage, can you pay for the level you're looking for? Hint: Don't assume you will no longer get benefits if you reduce your work schedule. More than 60 percent of moms I spoke with were employed by a company and about 20 percent of those moms shared that they still received benefits with a reduced schedule because they achieved the right level of hours to keep their benefits. Only a few had to pay more for them.

- Do you have any benefits such as vision coverage or daycare reimbursements (full or partial) that will be impacted by a transition to part time? If so, how quickly do you need to utilize those funds or reimbursements?

- If you have vacation or sick days accrued, how will a transition to part-time status affect that time?

- If you lose benefits through your employer, what does the benefits package look like through your significant other? It's not only the cost, it's the premium and coverage, especially for any known conditions.

- If you plan on getting pregnant again, how does part-time status affect maternity leave?

- What tax implications, if any, exist if you change your career approach?

- What is the long-term impact of transitioning to a part-time approach to your career? For example, what happens if you think you will transition to part time for a while and then decide that part time is your thing and you don't go back to full time again? How will that impact your long-term financial and retirement plans?

Additional Financial Questions for Entrepreneurs

On top of many of the questions that employees should think through, entrepreneurs have more areas to consider. If you're starting a business, there is often a degree of uncertainty, especially at the initial stages. And this can be the case, even with seasoned professionals who have strong networks, as I saw in my interviews. There are benefits to being an entrepreneur though, including a potentially much higher hourly rate. This makes understanding your own situation that much more important. Speak to a tax professional or financial planner to understand the financial implications of your entrepreneurial endeavor.

- What are your expectations for business in the first year? In the first five years? How does this compare to your current full-time job salary?
- Do you already have potential clients lined up or even clients who have already agreed to go with you if you start your own company?
- If your significant other doesn't have access to healthcare through work, what will coverage cost you?
- Consider employment taxes (e.g., social security) as well as short-term and long-term disability.
- If you had life insurance through your employer, how will you get life insurance moving forward? What will it cost?
- Have you considered the tax implications of starting your own business?

- What are the costs to start up your own business in your state or city?
- What expenses will you have for tools and services to do your job?

In summary:

The financial aspect of transitioning to a part-time role is important to consider as an initial step. While there can be financial benefits to transitioning to a part-time role, it's important to understand the overall effect in your specific situation. When in doubt, contact a tax expert, financial planner, or even ask your HR representative.

- Understand your value based on your skills and experience.
- Consider the impact of a potential pay cut, both in the short-term and long-term.
- Understand the impact on your retirement plans.
- See what other financial implications might exist.
- Entrepreneurs may have additional questions and areas to consider.

CHAPTER 8:

ENTREPRENEURSHIP AND WORKING PART TIME

I WALKED YOU THROUGH financial questions, including ones specific to potential entrepreneurs. You might have looked through the questions for entrepreneurs and wondered about starting a business to work part time. I'm including information on what to start thinking through as it relates to entrepreneurship, including various aspects that have come up in the interviews and in more recent conversations I've had with moms who started a business.

Please note that this is not a chapter on the step-by-step process to start a business. There are many resources available to walk you through that available in the marketplace. Take a look at www.mompowerment.com for links to those resources.

Entrepreneurship Statistics

You're pondering about starting a business. Answering the questions about the financial side of entrepreneurship got your wheels turning even more. But what does entrepreneurship look like across the United States? Here are the quick facts to consider about small business in the United States:

Entrepreneurship is vital to the U.S. economy. There are almost twenty-nine million small businesses or about 99.7 percent of U.S. businesses, according to a 2016 report from the Small Business Administration.[1] Those small businesses employ almost fifty-seven million U.S. employees, which translates to about 48 percent of the private sector workforce.[2] To break that down further, "Established businesses with fewer than 50 employees make up almost 68 percent of all employer firms in the U.S. and are a source of local economic activity."[3]

A report commissioned by American Express OPEN estimates about 38 percent of small businesses in the United States are majority-owned by women, which translates to over eleven million businesses and almost nine million employees.[4] From an economic perspective, women-owned businesses are generating more than $1.6 trillion.[5]

You might be wondering how women-owned entrepreneurs do when they start their businesses. In 2016, First Round Capital, a venture capital firm that invests seed stage money in start-ups, provided lessons learned after ten years in business. The company found that "investments in . . . companies with a female founder performed 63 percent better than [their] investments with all-male founding teams."[6]

Let's talk mom-owned businesses, since this book is all about moms. Of the women-owned businesses out there, it's estimated that one in three are owned by moms.[7] If you do the math, that's more than three million businesses. That number is amazing! Moms are succeeding every day in starting and running their own businesses. It can be done – with a family.

Benefits of Entrepreneurship According to the Interviews

Maybe you're wondering what you get out of being an entrepreneur that you don't get out of working part time for an employer. You might be asking why even consider this as your next step or a possibility down the road. There is no doubt that being an entrepreneur can be hard work, especially in the initial stage. There are many benefits though, starting with building the business you want at your own pace while working part time. When I looked specifically at benefits from the perspective of mom entrepreneurs who shared their story, the number one benefit was time with family and number two was flexibility. More satisfaction with and happiness in their lives, more options, and balance round out the top five benefits. The financial side of things, where you can potentially work less and make more, does make the top ten list from the interviews, and is a major draw for some mompreneurs.

Is Entrepreneurship Right for You?

I have had my own business doing marketing consulting since the summer of 2012. It's interesting and hard work at the same time. It's not for everyone. I understand the benefit of working part time for an employer and as an entrepreneur because I've done both.

Now that you've looked at the questions for entrepreneurs from the previous chapter and read the benefits of having your own business, you're thinking about starting one. And the burning question is whether becoming an entrepreneur is right for you. As with other questions I've shared, I can't answer that but I can get you thinking about entrepreneurship in a different way to see if it's the right fit for you.

Almost 40 percent of moms who shared their stories with me started their own business when they decided to transition to a part-time approach to their career. Some people know they want to be an entrepreneur, even if it's years away, which was the case for some of the moms I spoke with. It was easy for them to know it was the right next step.

For other moms, their then employer didn't support a transition to part time or clearly didn't demonstrate an understanding of work-life balance. Many of these moms looked at opportunities outside of their then current employer and still couldn't find what they were looking for, so they created what they wanted. It was the right time and they felt comfortable with their level of experience and depth of knowledge.

Uncertainty and Entrepreneurship

A marketing consultant for consumer packaged goods who works thirty hours per week in Dallas, Texas, shared that the "Risk and the first six months were brutal, in general. I felt pressure and uncertainty because I had no history [as an entrepreneur] initially, even with a lot of experience in corporate America." She's now been an entrepreneur for more than three years and is sought after for her skills and knowledge. She suggested getting your financial ducks in a row before starting your business and being mentally and financially prepared for the potential financial risk.

Can you handle if it takes time from a financial perspective or if there are inconsistencies? Is the risk at a reasonable level or does the financial uncertainty make the overall risk too high? If it does, then entrepreneurship might not be for you.

Let's be honest, not everyone is open to risk. There is the potential for uncertainty for a while when you start a business. You might get clients lined up right away or it may take time. "My biggest challenges are not knowing the future and what my next project will be," shared a consumer packaged goods consultant in the Minneapolis area. Many people are risk averse. If this is you, maybe entrepreneurship isn't for you and that's OK because there are plenty of opportunities at an employer to find or create a professional part-time role that works for you.

Business Development and Problem Solving

It's not only about doing work for most entrepreneurs. You are always doing business development, which means you are selling, to some extent, almost all the time as you create a pipeline of potential clients. Yes, you can hire someone to do the selling, but I don't know many entrepreneurs who do that regularly unless they create affiliate programs.

Selling doesn't mean you must be a salesperson, but you do have to be comfortable talking to people online or in person about your business and what you can do for that individual or company. And that requires you to understand the problem you're solving for that individual or company. It's hard to sell anything, even if you're the best salesperson in the world, if you don't understand the problems you're trying to solve for potential clients.

Do You Have a Unique Idea?

You've decided you want to be an entrepreneur, so what is unique about what you're offering, whether a product or service? It might be your skills that make your perspective unique. It might be your experience that sets you apart. Whatever that unique element is, make sure you can articulate it to potential clients.

Do You Have the Right Tools?

Maybe you are thinking you can do what you do for your current employer as your entrepreneurial endeavor. For some, the transition to business owner is relatively easy, especially for industries with a low barrier to entry. Many entrepreneurs have access to all sorts of tools and resources, from low-cost marketing to shared meeting space to technologies that provide big-business tools at small business prices. Technology can help provide lower cost options and make your entrepreneurial journey easier.

What happens if you need specialized tools or resources? For example, if you're a surgeon, you can't simply decide you're going to do surgery on your own without the right resources such as a facility, instruments, staff, insurance, etc. That is an obvious example, but there are tools that you need for your business. You might have access to expensive tools at your employer that make your job easier. Can you get access to these as an entrepreneur without it being cost prohibitive? Is there something similar that is less expensive without impacting the strategic benefit? Think through the resources necessary, including financial ones that you need to start up your business.

Entrepreneurship – The Basics

You've thought through these initial questions and you're thinking that entrepreneurship is a good fit, so now what? Let's talk through the different elements that I recommend you consider as you build your new business.

The initial stage of starting a business will likely take time and effort, according to my own experience and that of the moms who shared their entrepreneurial journey with me. A marketing consulting, who works fifteen hours per week in the financial services industry in the New York City area, explained it well: "Starting something part time takes full-time effort initially."

My suggestion is to create some sort of business plan. This doesn't have to be 100 pages, but it's helpful to have something to be your strategic blueprint, even if it's basic. This is your guide when you set up your business or need to make new decisions. Check out www.mompowerment.com for links to a business plan template.

The Legal Side of Starting a Business

There are many layers to think through when starting a business. One of the places you can start is by considering the legal aspect of your potential new business. How will you set up your business (e.g., sole proprietorship, LLC, or S-Corp)? How you set up your company as a legal entity can impact your business from financials to benefits to liability. There are many online resources about this element or talk to a financial expert or attorney.

Financials of Entrepreneurship

Figure out financial information upfront, including your budget and understanding what you must do for taxes each quarter and year. Talk to a financial expert and/or look at online resources available to better understand the financial side of things.

A challenge that exists for entrepreneurs, but didn't come up in my interviews, is understanding the financing of your business. Do you need a large sum of money upfront to pay for resources, which includes paying someone to build your website? Do you need to buy online tools? If so, where will the money come from? That financing might come from your own pocket, family and friends, a loan from the bank, or even outside investors.

One of the biggest challenges for entrepreneurs can be inconsistent income. If you have your own business, whether you manufacture something or provide freelance services, you're ultimately relying on others for your income. And that comes with ups and downs financially and maybe even cycles, depending on your product or service. Not all moms are comfortable with inconsistent income. Do what you need to do to either become comfortable with the inconsistency or figure out how to have more consistent income.

Another area that can be harder for women is funding. While this is improving for females, women still don't get their share of investments from traditional resources. Don't forget about non-traditional options, though, where you can crowdsource funds from friends, family, and even reach out to your potential market for the product or service you're providing. And don't forget that businesses with a female founder historically performed better than all-male teams.[8] If you're looking for investors, regardless of the source, remember that finding initial funding may take time, even with the best business idea.

Define Your Product or Service

I mentioned earlier in this chapter that you need to figure out the problem you're trying to solve. Once you know that, you can start to develop the product or service you're creating. This can be as simple or complex as you need it to be. Use your own knowledge of your industry and potential clients to figure out the right level of complexity.

Consider Your Ideal Client

Ultimately, you want to play to your strength when you develop your niche. You might be saying you want everyone as a client, but I don't recommend this approach. When you try to appeal to everyone, you don't focus on anyone. Build your products and services with a specific niche in mind and go after that specific kind of client. You can become the go-to person for that niche and be incredibly successful.

Focusing on a niche requires you to have deep understanding of that smaller market within the larger marketplace. That includes monitoring if those needs change over time. If so, make changes to the products and/or services you provide. If you can't meet their expectations, they can go elsewhere. If you need to learn new things, take time to attend conferences or take in-person or online courses. Make sure to include this cost in your budget and remember that it's usually an expense you can write off.

Know Your Competitors

You figure out the problem you want to solve and your ideal client and you're set, right? Not quite. You need to understand what your competitors are doing. Do some research online. Understand their approach and their strengths. What can you do to be different and have a unique perspective, product, or service that clients come to you to get instead of going to the competition?

For those considering a field that doesn't have a lot of competition, consider the substitutes that potential clients use. For example, you might want to start an online magazine and you think there isn't any other online magazine in that space, so you're in a good spot. Before you get too excited though look at what is in print in the same category. Understand where else your ideal potential client goes for information. Is there an annual conference that provides all the information? Are there key bloggers in the industry that attract your same audience? Substitutes are as important as competitors for many industries.

Marketing

How will you sell your product or service? Develop a plan to get the word out and attract your ideal client. It can be simple and doesn't require deep pockets. Or you can have a multifaceted marketing plan with a substantial budget. Figure out what will work for your business and niche and be realistic with what you can spend to make things come together.

Pricing

What is your ideal client willing to pay for your product or service? If you're not sure, ask people within your ideal client profile. Develop relationships with your ideal clients through online groups or through mutual connections. Or they may be people in your network already. Talk about your product or service and get their input. See if additional elements you plan on including to add value actually matter. Understand their budgets before you start pricing your product. While your competitors might be a likely place to go to understand pricing, you might be putting out a different level of product (e.g., more value-based or a premium version), so that pricing might give you some ideas or it might not be helpful at all.

Being a Successful Entrepreneur

Create Structure

Life as an entrepreneur is easier if you're organized on the professional and personal side. Moms talked about organization and creating structure as it relates to their workspace, calendar, and time management. They recommended keeping things consistent and easy to find. It saves time and effort if it's all organized. Plus, at least in my case, it's also less distracting. I have a hard time working at home when things are all over the place.

As an entrepreneur, you likely have flexibility on where you work if you're not heading into an office every day. Figure out your rhythms and plan accordingly.

Create the Right Schedule

Understanding how your time is best used can be incredibly important for your short- and long-term success as an entrepreneur. Think through how you work best and schedule your time with that in mind. Understand how you work – your natural rhythm – and even where makes a difference in your productivity and overall abilities. Make sure that your work hours help you be most efficient.

As you build a business, it can be long and hard work. Consider your needs and those of your family and include them in your schedule. You might think about the long-term time with family, but don't miss out on the short-term in the process. Find the right tools or team members to help with things like project management, which can help with managing your schedule and timelines.

If entrepreneurship is something you'd like to take a stab at, I will share this final thought specifically about starting a business. A mom who owns her own advertising and sales company in Austin, Texas, shares these encouraging words: "Take control of your destiny because you can make your own path, especially as an entrepreneur."

In summary:

There are various aspects to creating a new business as an entrepreneur.

- Decide if entrepreneurship is something you're interested in.
- Understand the financial side of starting a business.
- Finding your niche in the marketplace can help you be successful in your business.
- Figure out your ideal client and understand how to market to that audience.
- Take time to get organized, which can be helpful for entrepreneurs, especially mompreneurs.
- Understand and implement the logistics, including organization and time management, necessary to set yourself up the right way.

CHAPTER 9:

PART-TIME WORK-FROM-HOME ROLES AND JOB SHARES

WHAT IF, AS YOU go through the questions in this section, you realize you need something a bit different in your role. Maybe your ideal role is a part-time work-from-home (WFH) situation or a job share. We'll take on each of these individually.

Part-time WFH Roles

About 30 percent of the moms had some sort of WFH element to their job. They worked in all sorts of industries, including law, marketing, engineering, real estate, and social work, to name a few. For some, it was because their homes were also the office for their own business. For others, they negotiated working from home with their employer for part or all their part-time schedule. If you're interested in this approach, this advice might help you create a plan for success in your own WFH situation.

If you're trying to talk to your employer specifically about a WFH role, a Gallup study from late 2016 shows that WFH employees are more engaged. There is a catch though. WFH employees are more engaged when they have face time as well. The study reports, "The optimal engagement boost occurs when employees spend 60% to 80% of their time . . . working off-site."[1]

Create a Physical Space

It's hard to ensure you get your work done when you don't have dedicated space, whether you work for a company or have your own business. The moms shared it doesn't have to be large, but it needs to be your space to get things done. When you go to that space, your family, including your young children, need to know not to bother you unless it's an emergency. Don't forget to define emergencies with your kids if they're at home and you need some time in your work space.

Don't Get Distracted

Moms who are considering working from home so that they get more household duties done during the work day should beware of distractions. The moms who described themselves as successful in work–from-home situations talk about not getting distracted by household duties.

From my own experience, I would also suggest trying to keep your house organized. I'm very distracted by stuff everywhere, especially stuff I see regularly. I need to keep the house somewhat organized to remove that potential for using my time to straighten things up instead of doing work.

Find your Natural Rhythm

We all have natural rhythms, especially when it comes to work. You know when you're more productive naturally. For me, it's in the morning. I have many friends who are night owls. Figure out what works for you and use that time as efficiently as you can. Make that your most focused time. And, especially if it's in the morning, don't get distracted by your email or to-do list.

In addition to your own natural rhythms, a jewelry-maker in the Boston area suggests, "WFH moms must consider the needs of their family." We can't work in a bubble, so think about your kids' natural rhythms, especially if they're young and not yet in school. This might make childcare even more important if your kids are most wanting interaction when you are naturally most productive at work.

The mom who makes jewelry in Boston also suggests creating a workday routine, especially to get things going in the morning and to keep you motivated. There are distractions, so you want a routine to keep you on track and moving toward your goals and deadlines.

Systems and Tools

In addition, something that has helped in her jewelry-making business is to create daily, weekly, and monthly to-do lists, using tools, which keeps her workflow on track. Other moms I know who WFH in a full-time capacity use physical tools like white boards or even a wall with special chalkboard paint in the area where they work. Many moms, including me, write everything down in a notebook. And there are certainly plenty of online tools, which are inexpensive.

Find the system that works with your own work style. Since the tools vary from mom to mom when they WFH, I include a list of updated resources I use and that other moms recommend at www.mompowerment.com.

Childcare

The WFH moms I spoke with shared that when you work from home, you still need childcare. If their kids weren't at least elementary age, moms expressed the need to either have someone watch their children at home or take their children to another location for childcare. In some cases, moms took their children to a daycare or preschool. In other situations, they were fortunate enough to have family nearby or even did a trade-off. A mom I interviewed took her kids to her sister's house one day a week and another day, the mom watched her own children and her nieces and nephews. Other moms had a caregiver, like a nanny or babysitter, who was paid to take care of the kids in the home.

If you're considering WFH, you must also consider childcare. You might have the sort of child who can play patiently for hours by herself or himself or with a sibling. Chances are that's not the case. I confess I have only heard stories of these children; mine are nothing like this. Even if they can entertain themselves, you might be listening to ensure your kids are safe or not making a huge mess. If you can't focus on work, you're not going to be at your most productive level and your work will take longer, which takes away from your family time. It becomes a cycle. Childcare can help break that cycle.

If you have limited childcare, consider your work schedule. Can you divide up your day so that you work in the morning before kids are up, and in the evening once kids are down? Working in the evening is how I extend my day a few hours. Can you work during naptime? If so, you need to know exactly what you're working on before naptime so you can fully utilize that time. For more ideas on productivity, check out Chapter 16.

Showcase your Achievements

A mom who had several WFH situations and is now an executive director of a nonprofit in Austin, Texas, working about thirty-five hours per week, shared that moms need to show their productivity levels, achievements, and overall value. Recognize and share your patterns of excellence with your manager and senior leadership. Set goals, based on your own thoughts and input from your manager and/or senior leaders that build to bigger goals and align with your strengths.

If you're not sure about how to do this, talk to other moms who might be in the same situation and see what's working for them. You might now know other moms who are in your local area who WFH, but you can find other moms in online communities. Do some research to find these groups or specific women within groups.

In-Person Time with People

Several of the moms who WFH talked about the need to meet with people in person when possible and when it makes sense. An Atlanta-based education consultant, who is a self-described extrovert, talked about feeling isolated since she works from home. She preferred the office setting, where team members can interact with each other. She is more able to get things done and most of her colleagues work from home, so this approach is usual for her team. Interacting with people in-person has helped her deal with the feeling of isolation and has helped her maintain a sense of connection with her clients.

If you have clients who aren't local, try to do at least some of your interactions through an online tool where you see each other face-to-face. It doesn't have to be every time, but at least a few times a month. It helps to maintain a connection. Perhaps you can use these online tools to present new work to clients to help you gauge their reactions. These face-to-face interactions can also help overcome challenges and moments of friction.

These same face-to-face tools can be used with a virtual team. It's helpful to have those virtual conversations instead of doing everything via email or even phone. It might take longer, but it's worth it. We can look at people in the face and see what's going on. At least in my experience and that of moms I interviewed, it's easier to build connections when we have face-to-face conversations at times.

The moms in the group who WFH also talked about the need to network. Networking is a key element of moms who work or want to work part time, with more than 30 percent of moms I spoke with giving this piece of advice. It's especially important for moms who WFH so that there is an in-person network to turn to for questions and connections, or even something as simple as a colleague to do a working playdate. (I share more about Networking in Chapter 14.)

WFH as a Temporary Situation

You might be considering negotiating WFH as a temporary stage of your professional part-time path. Maybe it's a good option as you're coming back from maternity leave. Or maybe you have a specific situation that needs attention in the next few months (e.g., bed rest, dealing with a family member's illness, etc.). A director-level social worker in Michigan, who works about thirty hours a week now, started working from home after a six-month maternity leave. She started back at eight hours per week. Initially, her team came to her house for in-person meetings. She would work for a few hours and then nurse her twins and then start working again.

Setting Up Your Job Share for Success

I interviewed two moms who either are or had been in a job share at one time. If you're looking at this scenario, these tips can help with your own job share situation. From a business perspective, a job share can be helpful in training new employees.

A mom, who job shares as an OB-GYN in Austin, Texas, described her job share experience as "a gift. I do what I love and I show my family that I love them."

Find the Right Partner

The Austin-based OB-GYN discussed that finding the right person to do the job share is integral. This is especially the case in her situation because she leaves her patients in the care of another doctor several times a week. It's by design in this case. She and her job share partner are on the same page and "mesh philosophically." The two partners have a similar approach to and philosophy on patient care and medicine in general.

This isn't just the case in medicine; you need this for all businesses. You want to partner with someone who thinks the way you do, interacts with team members with a similar mindset, cares for customers (whether internal or external) with the same approach, and addresses challenges that come up in a similar way to how you would. It's not going to help either side if the approaches of the two partners are completely different. Imagine the friction that would happen if each partner wants to take a different approach and goes down that path during the time he or she is in the office.

Communication

A key element to success is communication. In the case of the OB-GYN, she and her partner share information on all their patients. Before one is out of the office, she shares all information on patients so the other partner has easy access in case anything comes up.

Logistics

Another element, mentioned by moms who job share, is logistics. Both partners and management need to agree on hours and an overall schedule. The OB-GYN partners define schedules every two weeks with any major dates like vacation or conferences agreed upon months in advance. They are part of a larger practice, so their dates impact many other people as well as each other. They must coordinate their two schedules along with their support team and then among the larger group for coverage as an overall practice. It's a layer of complexity, but it works. For the OB-GYNs, each of the two partners gets a specific consistent day off and then they plan the rest of the time, checking in to compare schedules every two weeks to make sure there aren't any changes.

As you're planning your job share schedule, consider overlapping time in the office. This allows time to hand off projects or information and answer questions or discuss potential challenges coming up. It makes the job share much stronger and more productive as a team, not to mention easier.

In summary:

- If you realize that working from home or a job share might be a better fit for you than a simple professional part-time role, there are ways to set each up to ensure you're successful in these new roles.
- Consider various aspects of each scenario and include them in the proposal from Chapter 12.

PART III:
SETTING YOURSELF UP TO SUCCEED AS A PPWM

CASE STUDY: You Can Be High-Performing and Integral to Your Team, and Work Part Time

When she was pregnant with her first child, the petro-chemical engineer was running a plant, a role which would be extra challenging with an infant. The engineer and her manager agreed that she would transition to another role after maternity leave, at which point she would be working part time.

Over the past eight years, she has worked in various areas of the large petrochemical multi-national company. She is currently working in an IT role. The company was willing to keep growing her skills and enable the work-life balance she was looking for to make sure she stayed with the company.

Why transition to a professional part-time role? This engineer wanted her kids to feel like they got enough attention from their parents, so that was her main motivation for working part time. She had the flexibility to do different activities and help her girls grow academically, even when they were young. She taught them to read and how to do basic math. They worked on writing and had frequent visits to the library.

She recognizes that moms before her created the path to working part time. She suggests that even if no one has created the path at the company where you work, it never hurts to ask. After all, if you don't ask, the answer is no and you won't be working part time.

Her advice for anyone interested in working part time:

- *Intentional networking.* Be specific with your networking. Make your time count in these conversations.
- *Know where you can shave off time.* When not having intentional interactions, socialize less at work or eat at your desk. Part of being more efficient with your time is being organized.
- *Create a win-win scenario.* Make sure both you and your team and senior leadership feel like the part-time work approach is a good thing.
- *Understand what help you need at home.* You can find people and services to do all sorts of things. Be specific with what you need and go find the person or service to feel your need.

CHAPTER 10:

HOW POPULATION SHIFTS AND GENERATIONS IMPACT PPWMS

You've thought through whether transitioning to a professional part-time role is the right thing for your situation and you think it is. Whether you choose to continue to work for an employer or start your own business, increasing your knowledge and awareness of what's going on in workforce in the United States lets you see the full picture and gives you context. Consider what's going on, how your needs fit, and understand what's already worked or needs to be tweaked. You can look at how companies are benefitting and reacting. And that gives you better negotiating power and a greater likelihood for creating win-win scenarios with your employer or client(s).

The Impact of Baby Boomers

Working Baby Boomers

I mentioned early in this book that 10,000 Baby Boomers turn retirement age every day.[1] You might be wondering if that affects you. It does affect you, either directly or indirectly, and it's not necessarily an immediate effect.

Even though 10,000 Baby Boomers turn retirement age every day, it's unlikely they all will retire as they turn retirement age. Let's face it, not everyone who turns retirement age can retire because they might not be financially ready. Or maybe they don't want to leave the workforce. If all Baby Boomers who turned retirement age left the work force we would not have enough people to fill their roles. And imagine the institutional memory that U.S. businesses would lose if all Boomers left all at once. For now, we need Baby Boomers to stay in the workforce.

Some might point to technology taking over the jobs that many Baby Boomers would leave behind. While automation and technology will play a role over time, it's a long-term strategy for business. It's not going to happen overnight because of the level of effort investment required — both capital and resources. According to the 2017 McKinsey report, automation will happen, but it will likely be decades to see the full impact.[2] It also turns out that machines will likely take over parts of roles and few entire roles or occupations.[3] This is still a long way off. What will happen between the time that Baby Boomers do start retiring and automated roles becoming the norm in U.S. businesses? How will U.S. businesses fill those roles in the short- and long-term while automation becomes more commonplace?

This is where moms like you could fit in. Part of a potential solution to this challenge of Baby Boomers retiring and technology taking over is keeping more moms in the workforce, so that U.S. businesses don't have disruptions. Better yet, we need SAHMs to reenter the workforce. And, yes, some SAHMs will naturally reenter the workforce over time, as they see less need to be at home for their children. We need more skilled SAHMs coming back to the workforce though, and more educated, skilled women to stay in the workforce after having their first child or second, as it turns out. We want moms who have been working to come back from their maternity leaves and be successful and continue to rise through the ranks. Having work-life balance initiatives in place, such as part-time professional roles, will help with both SAHMs reentering and current working moms who are looking to work less.

And, why not use the opportunity for Baby Boomers to partially retire and be paired with a PPWM? In my talk at TEDxSMU Women, I described the example of pairing a Baby Boomer who wants to partially retire with a mom who wants to work part time. It fills the business' need and allows for training on-the-job with one solution.

Care for Aging Baby Boomers

Baby Boomers retiring could also become more of a challenge for working moms. I shared in Chapter 2 that working moms are getting sandwiched as they care more for aging parents. And while this is something that we need to change so that this care falls on both women's and men's shoulders, it's likely that for now, women who are often already moms take on this role. If companies want to make sure that moms aren't squeezed so much that they leave the workforce, they need to create more opportunities like professional part-time roles.

The changes related to Baby Boomers are fast approaching, if they're not here already. If this scenario sounds familiar, you're not alone. Starting that conversation can open the dialogue for a lot of women and moms in your company. Even better, come together as a group to have an open, honest conversation with senior management about necessary changes to accommodate the challenge of caring for aging family members. If more moms talk about this type of challenge, the company will start looking at solutions for a large group, instead of many private conversations between moms and their managers about each situation.

Millennials

Millennials create another layer of the work-life balance conversation. It turns out that part of what sets Millennials apart from previous generations, as it relates to this book, is that they start their careers looking for work-life balance, and not necessarily because of family obligations. In the Millennials at Work/Reshaping the Workplace survey done by the consulting firm PwC, 95 percent of Millennial respondents described work-life balance as important and 70 percent said it was *very* important. [4]

It turns out Millennials are interested in work-life integration, blending work and life together instead of trying to balance the two separately.[5] And a driver behind that is flexibility and using technology to enable all of these things to come together.[6] For example, they want to work several hours and then leave the office to go workout, spend time with friends, participate in a hobby activity, learn something new, or spend time with friends, and come back to work afterward.[7]

Millennial Mom Interviews

I spoke with several moms from the Millennial generation. And their stories, especially for the moms who are entrepreneurs, were different from those of the Generation X moms in their approach to motherhood and combining career and family.

One Millennial mom in the Boston area shared that she had an etsy shop and worked full time for several years and then resigned, so that she and her fiancée could travel around South America for five months. And when she came back, she didn't go back into the workforce. She focused on building her Etsy shop business so that she had flexibility for her future family instead of working really hard for a few more years and then pulling back once having kids. She works about twenty-five hours per week in her business.

A Millennial mom, who owns a children's clothing boutique and entertainment venue in Brentwood, California and works twenty to thirty hours per week, shared, "my family is embedded into the store" and "entangled in my business." She describes the two as "intertwined."

Another mom who does creative design and branding near Denver, Colorado, explains that life isn't quite so divided. She describes it as a "messy blend of work and family." That approach works for her and many from her generation who I've spoken to since.

Millennials in the Workplace

Millennials' influence on the workplace is just getting started. As of the first quarter of 2015, Millennials became the largest generation in the workforce.[8] Their needs will influence businesses to think differently about how to engage employees and provide meaningful work and time for family, both of which are important to the Millennial generation. Offering professional part-time roles is one approach that companies can provide to meet the needs from this generation. And that helps all moms in the workplace, not only Millennial moms.

Millennials are also starting to become managers who will likely welcome different approaches to career that offer more work-life balance, such as professional part-time work and remote or flexible work arrangements. As managers and decision-makers, they could also create the same for their teams or employees. Millennials can change the workforce based on their own interest in work-life balance, especially as they also start becoming moms and struggle with their own needs at work and home.

Generation X Moms in the Workplace

You can find a lot of information on the needs of Baby Boomers and Millennials in the workplace. It feels like there are countless articles and people who present themselves as experts on those two generations. What you don't find a lot of information on is Generation X in the workplace. However, there is lots of information on Gen X moms as consumers since they represent a powerhouse of spending opportunity from the perspective of brands.

I admit that I was intrigued by the information on Generation X that I found. Gen X is my generation. I saw so much of my own perspective and underlying beliefs explained. My draw to work-life balance, and that of my friends and colleagues and so many of the women I interviewed, made more sense. The research findings helped me understand how we're not alone in how we look at work-life balance. And, since it's rare to find this information spelled out in easily accessible places, I thought it was important to include it here.

Gen X is sometimes called the "forgotten middle child," especially since it's less vocal and smaller than the generations that bookend it.[9] And yet, Gen X has come up with countless advances for women along the way. According to Hannah Ubl, a generation expert at Bridge-Works, a generational consulting company, "It was Gen X women who paved the way for work-life balance–maternity leave, nursing rooms at work, [and] flexible hours."[10]

Part of why Gen X women are different than their Millennial and Baby Boomer counterparts is that "Gen X women have more life challenges [going on],"[11] says Tacy M. Byham, PhD, CEO of Development Dimensions International, a global leadership consultancy. She shares that, "Millennial women may or may not have kids, but gen-Xers have kids and aging parents. Those life circumstances become a barometer for where they want to go and how fast."[12]

Simply based on age, experience, and education, Gen Xers are often in middle to senior management positions at work at this point. This might be precisely where you find yourself as you're contemplating a new position, which will result in a lot more hours at work and/or maybe you'll find yourself more stressed because of more responsibility. And that's not necessarily what you're looking for at this point of your life.

There is the idea that "strong commitment to family prevents them from going after a promotion, because they feel they need to take care of their kids or their elderly parents first."[13] Where does this need come from? What makes these moms maybe even take a break from their careers as they focus on family, whether their children or parents?

In large part, the answers seem to be from the environment that Gen Xers grew up in. Think back to your childhood. Maybe you were a "latchkey kid," one of the countless kids who had a key around your neck to let you into your house because *both* parents were working. Gen X was the first generation where this was common.[14]

According to BridgeWorks, "Many Xers were left to fend for themselves after school. As many as 40% of Gen Xers were latchkey kids. . . . They learned to be independent early on. . . getting their homework done. . . and no one was hovering over them. . . ."[15]

And today, we still don't need that push from our managers and senior leaders. We make things happen in any environment, including WFH or in flexible schedule arrangements, because that's what we do. With that in mind, we expect our managers and senior leadership to trust us to get things done without being under their watchful eye.

Gen X moms are also specifically looking for work-life balance. They "reject the notion that more hours in the office [equals] a more productive, hard-working employee."[16] They will be incredibly productive to do whatever it takes to get to their child's activities and to focus on family after work hours.[17]

Having it All

Gen X women were constantly exposed to "the women's movement," in which we saw constant examples, even in commercials on television (in the days before people skipped ads) where women could have it all.[18] I'm not alone in thinking I was sold a bag of goods about having it all. I can't count the number of women I've spoken to who work full time and have said that it's not really possible to have it all. And I will say, that based on the common version of having it all, that's true.

And that's the key to Gen X. We want this focus on family and we want to succeed at work. We're willing to change what "success" means so that we have it all.

Considering all the things that Gen X has already done for women, we're clearly willing to make advances for other women as we go. We're working on redefining what being a working mom looks like for ourselves and the women moving up the ranks behind us.

Gen Xers and Entrepreneurship

I've talked about women in the workplace largely as it relates to women at employers. What's interesting is that many Gen Xers are entrepreneurs. When you think of a start-up, you might have the image of a bunch of twenty-somethings with a new, brilliant idea often related to technology. Most people I've spoken with think of young people when you say start-up. According to a 2015 study by The Sage Group, a software provider for small and medium business, about 55 percent of starts-up are Generation Xers. That same study shows that 57 percent of start-ups are founded by women, largely for more work-life balance.[19]

According to Bridgepoint, "[Generation X is] leading the workforce as innovative. . . contributors, and are at the forefront of some of the most disruptive workplace shifts we've seen to date."[20] Generation X has been bringing innovation into the workplace for some time. It's how we think. This ability to think outside of the box (because, really, who has time for staying in a box) is what makes Gen X moms an integral group to bring a new way of working to companies and as entrepreneurs. With Gen Xers driving so much change already, sometimes below the radar with their head down and get it done mentality, it makes sense that Gen X will help drive the change necessary to make professional part-time roles normal and commonplace in businesses, big and small.

The Three Generations Must Combine Efforts

I've broken down what makes the three generations of women in the workforce special. In reality, we need all three generations of women and moms working *together* to drive change in the workplace. No generation can do it alone. Instead of using an us-versus-them approach, let's combine efforts as women and moms. Ultimately, we all want the same things; our approaches take us down different paths to get there. We can each play to our strengths so that we move the needle together. Doing so might make it happen faster and more easily.

In summary:

The three generations — Baby Boomers, Millennials, and Generation X — are all important to changes happening in the workplace related to more work-life balance for moms.

- As Baby Boomers leave the workforce, the roles they leave behind will keep more women in or bring back more women into the workforce.
- Millennials' interest in work-life balance as a pillar to their approach to work will influence businesses to integrate this into employees' lives.
- Generation X moms have been driving change and paving the way for change for all moms and women through the years and they must continue to lead the charge.
- The three generations must work together to make change happen in the workplace.

CHAPTER 11:

THE BUSINESS CASE FOR PPWM OPPORTUNITIES

NOW THAT YOU UNDERSTAND the mindset of the generations, let's briefly consider the perspective of employers. While this specific chapter is more geared toward women who will continue to work for an employer, this information is still helpful to entrepreneurs. And, if you're choosing to be out on your own, this might help you understand how to talk to others about your decision (e.g., your significant other and family) and how to position yourself with your clients.

Specifically, for moms who work for an employer, whether a small business or large corporation, we'll discuss information on what your employer is dealing with and how workplace dynamics in the United States will help your case to change your career approach. And, let's face it, understanding your employer's perspective and the workplace in general never hurts as you build your case.

Although I will be writing more about the business perspective and needs in a later work, I wanted to introduce two concepts. These two concepts shed a different light on the business side, which moms can keep in mind as they position themselves to transition to a professional part-time role.

Women in Senior Positions Impact Company Financials

In the study conducted by the Peterson Institute for International Economics (PIIE), Is Gender Diversity Profitable? Evidence from a Global Survey, Noland and Moran analyzed almost 22,000 global publicly traded companies in 91 countries and found a positive financial impact of women in leadership positions. Noland and Moran shared,

> When we examined the profitable firms in our sample (average net margin of 6.4%), we found that going from having no women in corporate leadership (the CEO, the board, and other C-suite positions) to a 30% female share is associated with a one-percentage-point increase in net margin — which translates to a 15% increase in profitability for a typical firm.[2]

Imagine the impact of this increase in profitability in highly competitive industries. And this is only one reason to keep women at a company over the long-term.

Cost of Replacing Moms Who Have Left the Workforce

Since we're on the topic of the financial impact of women, let's consider the cost of companies letting moms leave a company or the workforce in general. What if companies decide that they can simply replace the women who leave the workforce to become SAHMs?

What will that cost the company? The cost of replacing employees who leave a company is between 50 and 200 percent of their current salary with more senior positions tending to lean toward the 200 percent side of things.[2] This is the cost to find, hire, train, and get new employees up to speed. There is a time and financial cost as well as the impact of losing the knowledge and experience of the employee.[3] And those seasoned employees, or even more junior employees with high potential, might be going to the competition.

In summary:

It's important to consider the business need for PPWMs.

- There is a financial benefit to companies with women in top leadership positions.
- It is costly to replace working moms who leave the workforce, which will impact companies' bottom line in the short- and long-term.

CHAPTER 12:

THE PROPOSAL

I HAD SPRINKLED THE seeds about being interested in working part time in conversations about post-maternity leave in my own situation. While I didn't do a formal proposal, I was strategic in how I positioned a part-time role. There were many transitions happening at the time I went on maternity leave. Several weeks before coming back to work, I had a more formal conversation with my manager and we finalized when I would return to work and my hours. Looking back, I would have done things differently and put together a more formal proposal to better define my role post-maternity leave.

If you're like I was while working for an employer, you now know more about your employers' perspective and situation. So, how do you set yourself up for success from the beginning and over time?

Many moms I interviewed described themselves as high performers or overachievers. The moms who work for an employer were often in a situation where their managers or senior leadership were willing to consider a role with reduced hours because they didn't want the mom to leave the company. These moms were and still are an integral part of the team. And the company had invested time, energy, and money on these moms.

That said, these high-performing moms didn't bring up the topic of reducing their schedule or changing their roles in passing or in a random situation. Many of the moms talked about creating a proposal to present to managers, senior leadership, or whoever the decision-makers were, and setting up an appointment to present their proposal. They approached requesting this transition like any other strategic project or recommendation. And the driving force behind it was to provide a win-win situation so that both the mom and employer received benefits from this new career approach.

Strategically, it can be incredibly useful to go in with a framework of, "This is how I have already been successful for this company and how I will continue to be going forward." This is especially the case if you want to continue to move forward in your career. It's helpful to show how going part-time will in no way take away from your demonstrated track record of achievement.

The Decision-maker Perspective

As with any presentation or proposal, understanding the perspective of whoever is on the receiving end is important. Understand what makes them tick. Think through what will matter to them and how your request and recommendations impact them or their team(s). What kind of information does your manager or senior leadership always ask for when hearing a presentation? Be proactive in addressing what you think will be their concerns. Show you've thought through their perspective and questions. You can even say, "You might be wondering about how this impacts X person on your team," and then provide your recommendation.

A few moms suggested speaking to another manager to understand the perspective of a manager and have someone that can answer any of your questions. Even more helpful is speaking to a manager who has part-time employees on his or her team, to see what changes, if any, he or she made for that employee, what challenges have come up, and how those challenges were solved. If you think it might be helpful, see if the manager with experience with PPWM on his or her team can talk to your own manager about how this scenario is doable.

What to Include in a Proposal to Current Employer

Your proposal provides an overview of your proposed role, even if it's the same role with fewer hours. In addition to that, some moms laid out a detailed plan with a schedule and hours and how a part-time schedule would work. A mom in Long Island, who works about twenty-one hours per week for a small construction business, shared, "Propose a plan and create an action plan to make it work and say 'let's try this' and spell it out."

An Austin-based in-house attorney, who works thirty to thirty-five hours per week at a large technology company, shared that she wrote a proposal to "answer all her manager's and senior management's questions so no one could say 'well, how would that work?'" She included a schedule, a request to work from home one day a week, a transition plan, and an overview of communication, even when she worked from home.

The elements in proposals varied from mom to mom, so the following includes all the topics mentioned and a few more I would suggest you consider. You don't need to include all of them. If you're not sure of what to include, talk to other moms in the company or within your tribe who have transitioned to part-time roles and ask what they included.

Description of the Role

Describe what you want your role to be and how you want it to look. Be detailed. How are you changing your previous role? Is it a reduction in hours or are you creating a new role altogether? What effect, if any, will this have on your manager and direct reports? If you're taking on less in your current role, where will the rest of the work you previously did go? Who will take it on? Is he or she ready or is it a chance for him or her to grow? If you're proposing a new role outright, you still need to consider who will backfill your previous position or if it needs to (or can) go away.

How You Can Fulfill the Role

Provide information on why your background makes you ideal for this this role. If it's your current role with reduced hours, you can include information on being more efficient due to your previous knowledge and experience.

Schedule

Describe what your schedule will look like, including days you will work and the specific hours. This should reflect your childcare situation, so that you don't have to figure that out too after the fact. Include time in the office and away if that is an aspect you're proposing.

Why

Explain, to whatever extent you think is necessary, why you are making this request. When you write this, you aren't only explaining your perspective. You need to write this with your manager or senior leadership's perspective in mind, so it's unnecessary to share every detail of your why if you choose to include this section at all. Remember, you're creating a win-win scenario.

Timing of the Change

Explain timing on when you will transition to the part-time role. You might be ready to switch today, but all the moms I interviewed suggested a transition to the new schedule. It allows for your employer to make changes as necessary and you can make personal and business changes, preparing for the new schedule and potentially a new role altogether.

Communication

How will you communicate in this part-time role, especially when you're out of the office, if something happens? Address any changes to your usual communication approach. When you transition to a part-time role, you want to put boundaries in place, so that you don't have to be on call when you're not in the office. If you're in a role that won't allow you to completely turn off when you're at home, create boundaries with your team's, client's, and even manager's needs in mind, in addition to yours and those of your family. (I discuss more about putting boundaries in place in Chapter 17.)

Keep in mind that it's easier to set boundaries, especially as it relates to communication, upfront instead of trying to transition and then create this structure and these boundaries afterward. And some of these areas might need to be negotiated.

Transition Plan

Do things need to happen during your actual transition? Do you need training for a new role you're taking on? Do you need to train others on your role? Spell these things out, including timing, so that there aren't questions and things don't slip through the cracks. Remember that you will likely be managing this process. And, realistically, you probably want to be the one managing this transition, so enable your manager and senior leadership to entrust you with driving this change.

Metrics

Understand how you will be measured over time. Do you want to be measured against the same metrics as someone who works full time or if not, what adjustments would you recommend? Spell it all out. Make sure these are specific enough and make sense for your situation. Understand that this section might get pushback, so be able to articulate your reasoning and be open to changes from your manager and senior management. And, keep in mind that this might change over time.

Review Period versus Check-ins

Include reviews to ensure things are going as planned. Don't have major reviews too soon and don't wait too long. Ask around to see what other moms are doing. Most moms I spoke with talked about monthly or quarterly in-depth conversations.

Several moms I interviewed shared that they do check-ins with people on their teams, including their managers. For some moms, they're available whenever people on the team want to chat, but they meet weekly with their managers or key team members to make sure things are going smoothly. Recommend whatever timing makes sense in your situation.

Adjust as Necessary

Although it's great to have a plan, both sides might need some wiggle room to adjust elements of the plan over time, especially after a review period. Have your manager or senior leadership agree to both parties discussing any adjustments to understand the implications before they are finalized.

* * *

If you're specifically proposing a new role, you might also want to consider including the following instead of or in addition to what's included above:

What is the Need

You might need to pitch the idea for the new role you're recommending. Define why they need a new role. This is the time to show that you've done your research and thought through the needs of the team, department, or company, or all three. Explain how it will benefit the team or department.

Reporting Structure

If the new role is in a new group (sometimes you can take advantage of new opportunities), describe any structural elements that you've considered (e.g., who you might work for or who might work for you, etc.).

Why You're the Right Person for the Job

Everyone reading the proposal may or may not know you, especially if it's a new internal role. Explain how your background is the ideal match for this new role that you're recommending. Highlight your skills and expertise, as it relates to this new role. You don't want to be too cocky or overwhelming, but be thorough enough to leave no question about how perfect you are for the role.

As a bonus, a few proposal templates are available on www.mompowerment.com.

Timing Your Request

While some of us might have moments where we throw up our hands in surrender and quickly make changes at work, this shouldn't be the case here. Timing is something that came up several times in the interviews and something that moms need to think through as they consider or actually make changes in their career approach. Consider the existing constraints you have, which may be personal or work-related.

On the personal side, you have seasons like summer, when kids don't have usually have a set structure without registering for camp (which often happens months before summer). A transition before summer likely means a different approach to summer for your family. The holidays are another time that may require a different approach temporarily. Many people are out of the office, including clients, so you can start to work part time and figure out any kinks and be more ready for the full transition after the holidays. A director of operations, who works virtually from her home in San Antonio, Texas, about twenty hours per week, spoke to her senior leaders about transitioning to a part-time role when she realized she wanted to spend more time with her family during the holidays.

Another natural time to make the request is as you're coming back from maternity leave. You've likely been out for several weeks or even months. Why not come back to a part-time role? You can make your case while on maternity leave or even just before. Understand the implications of transitioning to a part-time role beforehand, since that could impact your status and eligibility for maternity leave.

On the career side of things, you might have several times in the year where timing matters. The two pieces of advice shared by several moms were: 1. Don't make changes before bonus time as this might affect your bonus; and 2. Consider timing on major projects at work. Are you part of a team with a major deadline, such as an important conference or negotiation for a deal? You want your manager, team members, and senior leadership to consider you integral to the team, especially when the time comes to propose a change in your schedule. That doesn't happen when you ask for a major change weeks before a major deadline and you leave the team in a bind. It also doesn't set the stage for a win-win type of scenario between you and your company.

If you find yourself needing to make a transition around these times, try to make it a gradual adjustment over time instead of an immediate drop in hours. And that still will likely keep you in a positive light with your manager and team.

It's a toss-up on whether or not to ask to transition into a part-time role during moments of major change at your company. For example, your manager or department head might change. Maybe there are some new major economic challenges. The uncertainty might hurt your professional situation or it might be an ideal time for change in your career approach. For example, when I made the request to transition to a part-time role when I worked for a large marketing agency, I sprinkled the seeds before maternity leave, but that was partially because the company was dealing with financial challenges. It made sense to keep me on, but not in a full-time capacity. Some managers might have said they needed a full head count and couldn't reduce the number of hours of anyone on the team because they had laid off staff. Essentially, you need to be able to read the situation and the impact on your team of whatever the uncertainty is.

Negotiation Skills

There is no question that negotiation skills become an integral part of the conversation for moms who want to work part time, especially as it relates to negotiating what you want and what you're willing to give up. Although few moms I interviewed specifically spoke about negotiation skills, they made a difference to a huge percent of the women I interviewed, based on the stories they shared. With that in mind, I want to take a moment to get moms thinking about how to be more productive in their conversations and negotiations with managers and senior leadership.

Understand Your Motivation and Value

Moms need to understand their motivation and value to have productive conversation and create a win-win scenario. The moms who did this could articulate their points without hesitation because they were prepared with this information.

Be Prepared

The more prepared you are for your negotiation, the better and more likely you are to be successful. The successful conversations and negotiations that moms shared were based on doing research and speaking with other employees at the same company and employees of competitors. Some moms tried to better understand industry norms. Many moms were creative in their approach to negotiating with their manager or with the company senior leadership. They understood the position of whomever they were negotiating with. These moms would consider both sides as they were asking for what they wanted, understanding any precedents and potential new policies that would need to be created.

Be Persistent and Patient

Sometimes it took more than one attempt at getting a part-time situation approved. Some moms had to wait to change managers or to change roles. The moms who didn't transition to working part time understood that circumstances can change and they didn't give up their desire to change their career approach. They were patient, waiting for the right time to make the request yet again. Changes are constantly happening, especially in industries that traditionally might not have had a focus on work-life balance. Be aware of what other companies or related industries are doing that you could use as an example moving forward, especially as it relates to business results or employee retention.

Trade-offs and Non-negotiables

Know what trade-offs, if any, you're considering. You will likely need to consider some, so prioritize them. Think through what's important to you in your personal life and what you want professionally. Put your trade-offs in order of importance.

Once you prioritize, you can better understand which trade-offs are acceptable and which ones are non-negotiable. Do a bit of research and analysis to create a list of non-negotiables from the perspective of your manager and your employer. The non-negotiables on both sides are a key element to your negotiation.

Know your Value

One of the most importance aspects of creating a win-win scenario and having a productive negotiation is to understand your value as an employee. Remove the emotional element and be able to discuss your value as an employee and contributor to the team and company. Many of the moms I interviewed talked about being high performers with years of experience. These moms were an integral part of the team, who the company simply didn't want to lose.

Several moms I interviewed advised moms interested in a professional part-time role to "know your worth." A consultant with a multinational company, who works about fifteen to twenty-five hours per week, put it, "Have confidence in your competence." Moms need to understand what they bring to the table, including strengths, expertise, and contribution to the team and company, both recently and over time.

Don't be afraid to tap into the topic of value when you eventually have a talk about salary. I mentioned that the financial aspect of working part time is often a challenge for PPWMs. As I shared earlier, when you reduce hours, that shouldn't immediately translate to a pay cut. Understand your worth to the company and present that information. Understand how your contributions impact the bottom line of the company and don't be afraid to bring this up as part of the discussion. It's the same kind of preparation you might do when you're about to ask for a raise. Instead of asking for a raise in the form of money, you're asking for a reduction of hours as your "raise."

If you're reading this book with the long-term in mind and want to increase your value in the eyes of your manager or senior leadership, take time to understand what your employer values. Long-term, where is the company going and putting effort? Does your skill set align with those areas? You will position yourself nicely for flexibility if you're in an area of tremendous growth or incredible importance to the company or even as an entrepreneur. It's not the usual way to think about long-term opportunities for part-time professional work, but it might be something you can do if you are looking at this book before you're even thinking about family.

Suggest A Trial Period in your Negotiation

If your manager or the company leadership seems hesitant, request a trial period. Put in place the way you will measure the results and what will be put in place based on achieving the necessary results. Again, this can create a win-win situation, where both sides learn and get their concerns voiced and addressed in the short-term so that it works in the long-term. You can use this as an adjustment period where you deal with any concerns from either side and then make a more permanent situation after the trial period.

A doctor of internal medicine in New Jersey, who works twenty hours per week in a private practice, suggested providing your expectations during the negotiation process on things like number of hours and days in the office. Her biggest suggestion was that it's easier to increase hours than it is to decrease time, so be prepared with the number of hours you want to work instead of trying to reduce your hours initially.

Should You Give an Ultimatum?

Many moms shared they were willing to leave the company if their request to get a reduced schedule was denied. This is an extreme approach to a negotiation and shouldn't be used lightly or as a scare tactic. If you approach the negotiation and have this as your ultimatum, be prepared for your manager or senior leadership to say "OK, go ahead and leave." This can happen, even to high performers who are integral to a team.

In summary:

A proposal could help explain your plan to your manager, senior leadership, and other decision-makers on how you can transition to a part-time professional role.

- Create win-win proposals, so that both you and your employer will continue to support the transition over time.
- Figure out what elements to include in the proposal.
- Write the proposal from the perspective of the decision-maker.
- There might be slightly different elements to include or not include if you're proposing a new role versus a change in your current role.
- Analyze and prioritize your trade-offs and think through your non-negotiables.
- Look at what's going on at your company now and in the future to understand timing of the request.

CHAPTER 13:

CREATE YOUR CAREER SUPPORT NETWORK

It's important to have a tribe you can speak with about your situation and challenges, regardless of what you want for your career at any given moment. It's great to have support from colleagues and those in similar roles. What other roles can provide support on this professional part-time work journey?

While support is often sought out by new mothers looking to work part time, those mothers who are having their second child may not recognize the need for it. Some women might say that they have already experienced life with a newborn, so they don't look for the additional help. I have two children, so I know what the transition from one to two can look like. I wish I would have sought out more honest conversations with friends or a mentor about the transition from one to two and gotten more ideas on how to prepare for it in my business and actually gotten the additional support earlier on.

I found that most of the moms I interviewed started looking for information and resources related to working part-time after the birth of a second child. It seemed that the sense of overwhelm often happened with the second child in most of the conversations I had with PPWMs with two or more children.

Mentors

Most moms I spoke with didn't specifically talk about mentors, but many shared that they talked to other moms who had already made the transition to part time at their current employer or in the industry in which they work or wanted to work. The moms talked to these other moms who had already taken the leap and might have even transitioned back to full time. These other moms whom they spoke with were further along in their careers.

A few moms even suggested talking to another manager to understand perspective and even word choice when dealing with her own managers. These types of conversations are similar to those you might have with a mentor. Mentors are important, especially to professional working moms who are interested in a part-time schedule. So, how do you make the most of relationships with mentors?

Take Your Time

You want to build these relationships over time, instead of trying to force an unnatural relationship. It's helpful to start having conversations before they become necessary.

Do what you can for career changes before baby arrives, including research, planning a career change, or thinking through reducing your hours. Even if you don't have the conversation with your manager or senior leadership, try having the conversations with others who can be mentors before your baby arrives. If you're concerned about doing this and your manager finding out, consider this as research, not a definite career change, as you look at your options. This is your chance to have the initial conversations and be mentored based on your needs, since there isn't some secret formula.

You might even decide after having the conversations that a part-time schedule isn't want you want. Maybe the conversations lead you down the path of asking for a WFH situation at your normal full-time schedule or even a flexible full-time schedule. And those kinds of a-ha moments are also part of the reason it's helpful to have the conversations before baby even arrives or before you return from maternity leave.

Now that you're thinking about the importance of mentors as you add to your family, how do you find and maintain a relationship with a mentor if you haven't had experience with one in the past?

Be Strategic

You want to find the right people to talk to. For example, talk to more seasoned moms who have already made the transition. Finding these moms who can tell you about their journey, including the ups and downs and ways to avoid mistakes, will help you get more out of your own transition. And try to talk to these potential mentors before you even go on maternity leave or better yet, even before you get pregnant, so that you can start thinking through their advice and figuring out what you need to work on ahead of time. You want time to integrate elements of their advice into your work or home life before baby has arrived. It's good to have space to look at your long-term opportunity at your employer or in your industry. And you have time to seek out answers to any questions you might have.

Another group that you can look into as potential mentors is those more senior people at your employer or in your industry, who are strong advocates of working moms, which includes men and women. They might or might not be parents, but they will have good advice for you as a future (or current) mom.

It's helpful to have more than one mentor and hear from a variety of perspectives. Even consider different levels of experience as well as different roles within the same department. It's like your own board of directors to provide strategic guidance about your career and that may include people at different career stages.

In addition to traditional mentors, you can also consider peer mentoring. This is similar to a mastermind of people at around the same level in their careers and journey. Fellow moms or moms–to-be might be dealing with challenges you've already dealt with or vice versa. Many of these tips apply for finding peer mentors as well.

- *Decide what you are looking for.* Understand what you want in a mentor and why. Ask yourself what questions you want a mentor to help you answer. Think through these elements before you even reach out.

- *Set goals.* Be upfront with what you want to achieve with a mentor. Decide what this looks like and how you will measure it, so that you can see if a mentor is meeting your needs (and vice versa).

- *Find a good fit for personality, style, and approach to career.* This is a professional relationship, but you want to make sure there is a good fit personally and professionally. You are asking this person for career advice and want to make sure your personalities and career approaches mesh. It's hard to ask for advice that you can follow if your personalities aren't even in the same spectrum.

- *Don't feel you must mimic his or her path.* You want someone whose advice you can follow, but you don't have to follow the same path. You might not even be looking for a mom or even a woman as your mentor. You can find someone who took a different approach to his or her career, but you want someone to provide strategic and sound advice on those things. This person might not have even transitioned to a part-time role, but he or she has colleagues and employees who have and can share insights on how to do it successfully. Or it might be a senior leader in the area in which you want to grow, so you ask about what being more senior looks like and that might help you better define your part-time possibilities.

Establish Communication Approach or Style

You've found someone to be your mentor, so now what? Put a few things in place initially, so that you can get the most out of the interactions.

- *When?* Decide how often you will meet. You might even put a few preliminary dates down on the calendar upfront since it might be hard to find time on his or her calendar. Be aware of how busy this mentor is before you ask for meetings that might be too frequent.
- *How or where?* Decide how you'll meet. If he or she is in the same city, do you want to meet for coffee or lunch? If coffee, is that first thing in the morning or in the afternoon? What happens if the person travels a lot and isn't in town on the date you picked? There are many virtual options for online face-to-face interactions or simply do a phone call. You have these same virtual options if the person doesn't live in the same city as you. Figure out the logistics upfront, so that questions won't come up later and that type of interaction is included on the meeting invite (e.g., online meeting log-in information).
- *Formal vs informal.* Figure out the style or vibe of the interactions and overall communication. This will be largely based on your own personality and that of your mentor. See what fits and what is needed based on personality, expectations, and schedules.

Tips to Get the Most Out of Each Interaction

- *Prepare for your interactions.* You want to be respectful of his or her time (and of your own), so ensure you prepare for your meetings, whether in-person or virtual. Do your homework and be prepared with your questions or challenges you want help with. Write things down so that you don't waste time trying to figure out topics to cover. And have notes for your own points that you probably won't share, but they give you more background or remind you why you might want to ask a question or provide context.

- *Consider sending an agenda or at least points you want to cover.* Send something beforehand to your mentor, so he or she knows what you'll be talking about. You especially want to send this if you think your mentor might want to do research or think through a past situation. An agenda is a must if your interactions are more formal.

- *Be engaged during your interaction.* Your mentor is largely there for your benefit. Make sure you use active listening skills. Ask clarifying questions. Be attentive and maintain eye contact. You want to clearly show you're listening and engaged.

- *Be open to constructive criticism.* Your mentor may see things going on that you don't and provide feedback. Listen to those insights and to the constructive criticism. The idea is to learn, so take full advantage of the relationship.

- *Follow up and say thank you.* Make sure that you follow up after the interactions and say thank you to your mentor for his or her time, insights, advice, etc. This is time away from other activities for your mentor, so show your gratitude. A simple email (especially if you're sending a link) or better yet, a handwritten note, is great. Talk about what you learned from the interaction. Follow up with anything you said you would provide such as a resource, article, or specific author or expert who your mentor might find helpful.

Finding the Right Fit

You've found someone that you'd like to call your mentor, but how do you know if it's the right fit for you and your needs?

- *He or she understands your needs and goals.* When you ask questions or look for advice from your mentor, does he or she clearly demonstrate an understanding of what you're looking for? Is the advice actionable in your situation or does it need to be adjusted a lot to be applicable or even usable in your circumstances? If the answers to these questions and the outcome is that his or her insights and advice help you overcome challenges or improve the outcome of your challenges, you have someone who understands your needs and goals and he or she is likely a keeper.

- *You have a new perspective or deeper understanding after you speak.* You are excited to meet because you're curious to hear his or her thoughts on a new potential opportunity or career challenge. You find clarity to help you with your challenges as a result of interactions with your mentor, which also shows he or she understands your situation.

Evaluate Over Time

Your needs might change over time and that could mean you need a slightly different mix of people giving you career advice. People might have less time to spend helping with your career decisions, or maybe you find someone who is a better fit for your specific needs in a specific moment. Maintain relationships with the men and women who have been your mentors, even if they are no longer in a mentorship role. You never know when your paths may cross again.

Give and Take

A mentorship is a two-way street. So, how can you help your mentor? Can you provide a perspective to a challenge he or she has? Figure out what you can help him or her with and do it. You want this to be mutually beneficial. Send an article you find on something he or she talked about. You might hear about an event on a subject he or she is researching. Share what you know about a topic you might know a lot about that he or she is starting to work on. Be generous with your time and knowledge and share what you find.

Final Tips for Successful Mentorship Relationships

There are a few more tips I suggest you integrate into this relationship that might result in an even better relationship with your mentor.

- *Be flexible.* It might be as simple as changing dates or switching to a virtual meeting to save time on a busy day.
- *Be proactive.* Figure out in which areas you can be proactive and do it. For example, send articles that you come across that you think might be helpful and connect the dots for your mentor instead of simply passing on an article.

Sponsors

Although I didn't realize it at the time, I often had a sponsor at the large marketing agencies where I worked throughout my career. They were often the senior lead on the team who were direct reports of the senior leadership team at the office or company. They saw something in me and were willing to give me access to new opportunities and help position my skills to new potential managers. I considered them mentors, but they were so much more than that. Now I know they were actually more like sponsors.

In larger companies, it's also recommended you seek out sponsors (this might also be helpful in larger small companies). Unlike a mentor, sponsors will promote your accomplishments and skills, help you make connections with more senior leaders inside and outside of the company, and help you get more visibility (e.g., recommending you for or engaging you on a new or existing high profile initiative).[1] Essentially, they're more action-oriented than mentors.[2] When it comes to moms interested in working part time, sponsors can talk to a manager or senior leaders about the need to keep a mom at the company, helping pave the path to a professional part-time role or to even helping create a role that allows for more work-life balance.

As an entrepreneur, you might be thinking that sponsors don't apply to you. Here's the thing – they do. Sponsors for entrepreneurs are different than those in a company, but they serve the same kind of purpose. These are people willing to give you access to their own network, but it's more than simple networking.[3] These are people who will open doors and make introductions with a seal of approval.[4] They might give you access to new customers or to investors, if you're looking for funding, who they know and might have done business with.[5] They could even introduce you to potential new members of your team.

Now that you understand more about the role of a sponsor and how it relates to PPWMs, the question then becomes how to find these sponsors who can be so helpful in your professional part-time work path.

Look at your Network

Analyze your current network to see if you have a connection who is currently a mentor at a senior level or was previously a manager or even a manager's manager. They might also be people who have left the company and are still highly respected. These are people who have moved up the ranks. It's helpful to find people who understand your role and haven't been in your shoes too long ago so they can still relate to your situation. These are people who need to be willing to take on a more active role in your career moving forward.

Look for senior people in your current network who have given advice that you have used and can show how their advice made a difference in your career or specific situation. If you've followed their example in your career, that is another element to share with potential sponsors.

Consider Previous Projects

If you've worked on a high-profile project in the past few years, consider reaching out to someone senior who seemed impressed with your work. He or she has already seen you in action and understands what you've done and what you're capable of. These men and women can see how you could help support their legacy at the company.

Create Opportunities to Work with Potential Sponsors

If you have someone in mind who you'd like to work with at your employer, try to create a situation where you can work together to show your skills and make the connection.[6] It can be hard to do at a company or as an entrepreneur, but there are opportunities to step forward and ask to be placed on a project with someone you'd like as a sponsor in the long-term.

Not sure how to make that happen? Find out what projects he or she is starting and see how your skills match up. Take the initiative and reach out to the person and say you'd like to work on his or her project because you think you can contribute because of your skills, expertise, and background, and you'd like to learn from him or her.

You can also get to know a potential sponsor outside of the office. This can be hard to achieve, but look at organizations that the potential sponsor volunteers with and find ways to get involved with that organization. It's even better if there are ways to volunteer that highlight your skill set.

What Can You Do for Your Sponsor?

As with any relationship, a relationship with a sponsor should go both ways. They too are looking at people to sponsor and want someone who can help support their long-term impact on a company.[7]

Are there elements to what you do, either within a company or with your new business, that can benefit your sponsor?[8] For example, as an entrepreneur, are you creating a product or service that might be helpful to your sponsor in some way, whether personal or professional? If you're at a company, can you provide some sort of support, such as giving perspective of the target market that your sponsor is aiming for with a new project? Essentially, can you help your sponsor achieve his or her goals for a new project? Do you have skills that might be helpful for your sponsor (e.g., social media or financial skills)? [9] If you're in doubt, ask how you can help support your sponsor and his or her initiatives.

In summary:

Outside of colleagues and your manager, there are generally two groups at work who form your support network: mentors and sponsors. Both can be helpful to an entrepreneur or employee who continues to move through the company ranks.

- Mentors provide guidance on your career decisions.
- Sponsors are more action-oriented when it comes to creating opportunities at work.

CHAPTER 14:

NETWORKING

WE'VE TALKED ABOUT SPECIFIC people who can help you achieve your goals and understand and analyze your potential career paths, so let's turn our attention to building our network. Why is networking important for PPWMs?

If you're reading this book, chances are you're looking to make a change from a full-time to a part-time role. As part of this transition, you may consider a new role at your current employer or a competitor. And that is where networking comes in. Networking is the most discussed topic and piece of advice from more than 110 interviews, with about 30 percent of the moms bringing up this topic in their stories and as part of their advice.

We often consider networking as we're looking for a new job, especially if we're looking to change companies. You might wonder why I'm talking about finding a new role at a new company if you're looking to transition to a professional part-time role. You can't find *new* professional part-time roles, can you? Actually, you can.

If you're trying to stay at the same company, but it makes more sense for work-life balance and professionally to change roles or even departments, you still need to network. It will likely be easier since a new potential manager can talk to people about you, your work ethic, and your work product. How will you find these other opportunities or how will they find you? It's generally through networking.

Of my interviews, almost one-third were with moms who found new opportunities outside of their then employer, which also includes a handful of moms who went from SAHM to part-time employee. If you want to look at this, comparing only those moms who are employees (versus the total group, which included entrepreneurs), about half of moms who were previously employed found part-time positions at new companies. Those moms who found positions outside of their employer suggested networking as their most common piece of advice.

And networking even helped the 38 percent of moms who started their own businesses. Their new businesses were usually in the same industry where they had been previously employed, so they needed to maintain their contacts. Their network could be potential customers or could open doors and make connections with potential customers.

The question becomes how to make the most of your networking, so that it's effective and efficient. Let's not forget that we don't have a lot of time as busy, working moms.

Networking as Intentional Interactions

When you hear the word "networking," you might think of large networking events where there is a lot of exchanging business cards. These can be industry events with a focus on specific topic or panels with industry experts. You often pay a hefty price for a ticket to attend. Maybe your employer sends you to these events to network with potential customers and suppliers or to hear more from your counterparts at your competitors. They might be close by and happen for an evening or a whole day. What about when they last several days, taking you away from family and changing up your family's routine? For some, this is a blessing and something they look forward to, but for many moms this is an inconvenience, even with all the benefits to your career.

From an online perspective, networking might make you think of the many seemingly random requests from people to join your online networks. How did they even find you, you might sometimes wonder?

The larger networking opportunities and the blindly reaching out or accepting online requests to join a network may or may not help you find professional part-time work. What will? Most moms talked about focused efforts, although having lots of touch points was certainly helpful to some moms.

A senior engineer at a large multinational petrochemical company shared that she does intentional networking. She doesn't have time for a random lunch with a coworker, but she intentionally makes time to meet with coworkers and industry colleagues at lunch once a week or every few weeks. That conversation and interaction serve a purpose. This engineer prepares for these interactions and knows what she wants to cover so that she can make the most of her limited time.

Have a Networking Plan

These intentional interactions get you closer to your short-term and long-term career goals. To be the most prepared, create a plan. You can include what makes sense. If you're specifically looking to talk to internal colleagues, your plan will look different than if you're looking for a new job outside of your company or industry.

Elements to consider for your plan:

- Keep in touch with your current network, both online and in person.
- Create goals on who to contact or number of contacts to make. Hint: give yourself deadlines to make sure you stay on target with your efforts.
- Define what you are looking for in your conversations (e.g., meeting people and extending your initial touchpoints, understanding a different company or industry perspective).
- Articulate your "ask" at the end of the networking session, if you plan on having this as part of your networking interaction.

Hint: Make sure that you don't force your agenda and your needs if it's not natural to the conversation. Maybe this is an initial conversation and another time you do more of the networking side of things with an "ask." Only you will be able to gauge this from the interaction.

- Know what you want to offer in return for whatever you're asking. And it can be as simple as asking "What can I help you with?"

Network Where You Are

Now that you're thinking about who to meet with, where do you find them? Do you attend those large industry events where hundreds or thousands of industry people come together for speakers and panels? They are great from a learning perspective and you can meet a lot of people who you might not have access to every day. You can even get access to industry experts who might be a keynote or a panel participant. On the other hand, they can also be expensive and time consuming, and the contacts you make might or might not be meaningful, based on your networking goals. Remember, you're aiming for intentional networking.

Let's say you attend one or two larger events a year, what about the rest of the year? Or what if attending a large event isn't something you can work in right now?

My suggestion is to network where you are. That way you have productive and meaningful conversations in more intimate settings. There are five places to consider for networking where you are:

- Meet with colleagues at your current employer in an informal setting
- Networking online
- Network with parents from your child's school
- Get to know your neighbors
- Chat with new people at social gatherings you're attending

Talking to Someone at your Current Employer

If you work for an employer, what about the built-in network of your colleagues? When was the last time you spent time with a colleague who you don't usually work with to hear what he or she does within his or her team or department? Probably not recently, if ever. In addition, most colleagues have worked somewhere else. Get to know these current colleagues and their stories in an informal setting like lunch or coffee and you can steer the conversation to learn more about their current and past roles and employers or any organizations he or she might be involved with.

You can also find out about their previous roles and initiatives in which they were involved. Whether they are more senior, your peer, or someone more junior, you can approach the conversation as a learning opportunity to better understand what's going on at the company and what they have achieved on their path at your employer, which is likely different from yours. You can learn about different managers, departments, initiatives, and even different locations. Networking is an easy way to ask about what teams or other departments are working on and learn more about positions, which might be ideal as a professional part-time role.

For example, what if you're a petrochemical engineer and you have decided that you need to cut back on your current schedule and know that probably won't work on your specific team. Maybe you want to be in a group that is more internally focused instead of at a production plant or global team that always seems to be on call. How will you find those other teams? Will HR give you that information? Will your manager? Is there an internal online toolkit? It's not likely that any of those is the case.

The easiest way to find these other opportunities at your current employer is to talk to other moms and, better yet, other PPWMs in other departments. Be specific with your networking requests and ask the questions. Find out firsthand about managers and team dynamics. If you're making an internal move to another group, you want your expectations to be in line with those of the manager and team.

You have the resources available to you. It's a matter of asking and finding the right people to talk to. If you're not sure who to talk to within a team, start asking around. Those moms with work-life balance often know other moms in the same situation in another department.

Or see what initiatives might be in place that focus on work-life balance and do some research to understand who heads up the initiatives or is highly involved. Those dialed-in individuals, normally women for women's initiatives, will be able to recommend someone for you to talk to.

Another topic to cover during these networking meetings is previous employers. You can understand the teams, departments, and initiatives at competitors or in related industries or fields. You might even find out about different industries. See what's different and what's similar. Ask why your networking partner left and if she or he would consider going back. Talk about what previous employers did in regards to initiatives for working parents or work-life balance or find out more on maternity leave policies and practices. Those initiatives and efforts might not be a match for someone else's needs, but they might be exactly what you're looking for.

Networking Online

People who you've worked with in the past have moved on and have moved away. They're still part of your network, but you don't have usual touchpoints with them. How can you maintain those relationships?

What about meeting people online? You're in an online group and you see comments from someone that seem smart and relatable. You do some digging and find out that the person is working in the industry or at the company that you want to know more about. He lives across the country though, so you can't meet. Or can you?

A friend of yours recommended you talk to someone she knows, but the person lives in another state that is six hours away. Sure, you could drive six hours if there is no other way. That's a huge inconvenience though, and something you'd like to avoid.

You read an article by someone at the company you're interested in, which resonated with you and what you're wanting to do. You want to know more, but the author is nowhere near where you live. Do you give up? Or is there another option?

You can have face-to-face meetings when it makes sense. And you can schedule phone calls. What about using technology to have face-to-face online meetings? Grab your cup of coffee or, if it's late enough, grab a glass of wine, and chat. You get to virtually meet and it's more personal than simply talking on the phone.

Sometimes you can reach out to someone on a platform to connect. Better still, reach out to ask them a question or ask to connect virtually in an online meeting. Some of the women I interviewed for this book were mentioned in articles and I reached out to them to ask if they'd be willing to share their story. It works. The worst that can happen is the person says "no" and the best is that you make a new, meaningful connection.

Networking with Parents at your Child's School

If you drop off or pick up your child from school, how often do you see the same parents? At least at our boys' schools, I see the same parents over and over.

How often do you talk to those other parents? How well do you know them? If you're like most, probably not very well. You say "Hi" and have light conversation in passing. These parents are a potential network though and you're missing out.

You might be thinking that the person is a SAHM or stay-at-home dad (SAHD) and isn't currently working, but you might not know the complete story. I work part time so that I can drop off and pick up my boys and it might appear that I don't work. Even if the SAHMs and SAHDs aren't currently working, most parents worked somewhere before kids. Maybe the parent previously worked in your field and has some insights about working part time. Maybe his or her significant other, sibling, mom, dad, or neighbor does what you want to do or works at the company you're interested in. Or maybe he or she has a unique blog or project going on that you don't know about. How will you know unless you talk to other parents for networking instead of light chatting?

So, how do you make that happen? There are a few easy ways to learn more about your fellow parents.

There are times when I'm volunteering with other moms and occasionally dads and we often talk about our kids and things happening at the school. Use the time as an opportunity to get to know the other parent better. If you're trying to move from chatting to networking, approach the conversation differently. Take a few minutes to talk about kids and related topics and then shift the conversation. Ask that person about work, education, etc. and use those responses as springboards for continued conversation.

What about at kids' parties when you're not simply dropping off kids? At most kids' parties, there is time when you're not totally focused on kids. Even at the parties that my three-year-old attends, it's not 100 percent focus on kids. I have time to chat with other moms and keep an eye on my child. Again, it's natural to talk about your kids in these settings, but why not ask, "What are you working on these days?" That can open the conversation to other non-kid topics and opportunities for networking. Keep in mind that maybe it's not the best idea to talk about work stuff at a child's birthday or maybe it is. You will know which way to go. Maybe it is your chance to schedule something another time. And, if it is a drop-off party, reach out to a mom or dad whose child is going and say you'd love to grab coffee while the kids are at the party.

Not sure how to transition to non-kid topics? Try one of these questions:

- "What do you do when your kids are in school?" If the answer to this is "I work" then the conversation should be easy to transition to non-kid topics after that. If the answer is SAHM or SAHD, then find other questions to help you understand more about life and career before kids.
- "Do you volunteer outside of school?" If so, ask about various aspects of that volunteer organization or the area of focus that the organization covers. That can be an easy segue into talking about life before kids, personal and professional areas of interest, and professional skill sets.
- If something like a holiday is fast approaching, you can ask about holiday plans. If they talk about seeing family, it's a great time to ask about family. How many siblings? Where do they live? What do they do?

The idea is to transition the conversation away from kids and start talking like adults, so that you can guide the conversation to how you would when you network, instead of chatting as two parents. And that gets them thinking of you as someone other than a mom at his or her child's school, which is helpful. You never know when parents from your child's school might come across opportunities that might be of interest to you moving forward.

In my case, I have gone from light chats with fellow moms to interviewing moms for my book, making countless professional connections, and even getting the opportunity to do some training. I even got ideas for the book and potential future courses and training, based on conversations with other moms where we dove into professional topics and things they felt were necessary or currently missing in the marketplace.

Keep in mind that only you know when the time is right to have the conversations and do the transition. If someone is clearly in a hurry, it's hard to have a real conversation, let alone dive into topics you want as part of a networking interaction. Don't try to have the conversation when you're both hurrying to pick up when minutes matter or when one of you is clearly trying to drop off and get somewhere. You can tell by his or her body language and pace of walking.

If you're both usually in a hurry, consider scheduling a coffee date or a walk after drop off, so that you can fit in some exercise while networking. If you choose the walking route, I recommend you take your phone to either record ideas you might get or to take impromptu notes. And let the other mom know what you're doing at the beginning of your walk so that you don't randomly grab your phone and start recording. A simple "I might record a few notes to remember specific points later" will let them know what's going on. Do not record the whole conversation but do jot down notes to remind you of a specific topic or a potential contact. If you want to take lots of notes, don't do a walk and try the coffee date route, where you can take a notebook.

The conversations can be very productive or they can be light. And look at cues that tell you whether to keep thing light versus trying to do more of a networking conversation.

Get to Know Your Neighbors Better

How well do you know your neighbors? If the answer is not very well, maybe it's time to get to know them. It can be as simple as taking over a treat, homemade or store bought, and knocking on the door. Mention you're trying to get to know your neighbors and would love for them to come over for the next breakfast treat or afternoon coffee date or whatever works. Maybe your kids are a similar age and they can play while you chat. You can even ask him or her to take a walk one morning or evening without kids. Or, if both sets of kids are stroller age, take a walk with kids in strollers. It's hard to take pen and paper with you on a walk, but similar to when you exercise with parents from your child's school, you want to be able to take impromptu notes.

Does your neighborhood have a playground or play area where you see parents with their kids? This is a perfect place to meet moms and dads. Start up a conversation and see what they do when they're not at the playground, playing with their child(ren).

In my neighborhood, there are many moms who work part time or with a flexible schedule, so we've chatted on the playground. We often start the conversation by talking about our kids and then shift to more professional topics. You chat with someone while your children play — a win-win.

Social Gatherings

All of us attend social gatherings, such as book club, happy hour with friends, or parties. Have you ever considered that you can network at these events, even though they're social time?

If you're in a book club, do the other book club participants know and understand your skill set or know what you might be looking for, if you want a change? Do you know what they do? I didn't know that a person in my book club was looking for a job for six months because she didn't ever talk about it. Why not? These people who you see regularly can be primed and ready as a network if we know each other's skills, areas of interest, and whatever we're looking for. In that same book club, do you know what their significant others do? If not, simply ask. You can even phrase it as "remind me what your husband does," if you think this topic has been covered in the past. The idea is to get people thinking about you in a professional setting. You never know when that person is talking to a neighbor, sibling, or even past colleagues or clients, and there could be a potential opportunity for the right role or networking contact primed to chat with you.

The last time you went to happy hour with friends, what did you talk about? Maybe you chatted about a challenge some of you are going through with kids or your significant other? Did you complain about your mother or mother-in-law? Those things are important and help you in so many ways on a personal level, so they should be part of the conversation. However, did you talk about professional stuff you're working on? Did you share a professional (or even personal) win? Something you're proud of that you want to continue in another way? Did you talk about the change you are trying to make professionally? Do your friends know you're looking to work part time? If not, why not? Aren't these the people most likely to recommend you to those they know? Talk to them about what you're looking for. It doesn't have to dominate the conversation, but you can start to plant the seeds about what you want. Ask them for an introduction, after you've done your homework about potential connections. You don't want things to be one-sided, so ask what they're working on, and figure out where you might be able to help them.

A huge benefit with happy hour and book club is that you don't have to put as much effort into transitioning the conversation away from kids. These are likely friends or at least acquaintances. They might ask a few things about kids and then it's easy to move on to more adult- and career-focused conversations.

And, what about getting to know the people who you don't know at the happy hour? There is often a tight group and sometimes there are new faces. Get to know new people. And it can be as simple as, "I don't know you yet. I'm _____." Simply start the conversation with the new person.

What about the holiday events you attend for your significant other or a charity you're involved in? It's a social gathering, where you can casually talk about your interests or learn from those around you. Make sure it's appropriate though. Maybe it's not the best idea to talk about work stuff or maybe it is. You will know which way to go. Or maybe it is your chance to make a connection and schedule a lunch or coffee. You probably have your phone so you can access your schedule.

And you never know where these connections pop up. I'm part of a small women's business group. We share ideas, give each other recommendations on resources, or respond to requests posted to the group page asking for advice. The first year I joined, I went to the holiday gathering at someone's house. I knew two people in the entire room and decided to mingle with others. I met a fellow mompreneur and, several months later, I worked with her on a business challenge she was having. And over the years, we've stayed in touch and met for coffee or lunch. She introduced me to at least four or five moms I interviewed for this book. They were past clients in her coaching business over the years. Would I have found other women to interview? Sure. But she was a great connection to some fabulous interviews and she was willing to open up her network when I shared what I was working on. And it all started because we spoke at a social gathering years ago.

You Know who to Meet with, but How do you get the Most Out of it?

You've got the networking meetings set up, but now what? Here are some ideas on how to prepare for those in-person or online networking opportunities and make the most out of the time and interaction.

Do your Homework

Regardless of who you're speaking with, do your homework. If you're lucky and you made the connection through a mutual contact, ask him or her for some initial information. If not, there are a lot of places to find information. Research the person's background, which can be done on LinkedIn or even Facebook, where people often list their current and previous employers and areas of interest. Or do a simple online search to see if he or she was mentioned in an article. If the person is involved in an organization, maybe she is also high-lighted on their website as a volunteer or activist.

You don't need to write a research paper on the person, but do try to be educated on the initiatives they're working on now and in the past. These are great topics to bring up during the chat if they pertain to the conversation. They're also great topics to help you understand steps this person took to get to their current level, department, or role.

Know What You Want to Cover

It's great to have natural flow to the conversation, where it organi-cally covers all the topics you might be interested in. It's more likely you'll get the most out of it if you prepare and have an idea of what you want to cover so you can guide the interaction. That way you can have some natural conversation and times where you guide the con-versation.

Maybe you want to talk about their current role, but what about it? Are you asking about how he or she got into that role, what he or she does each day, or a combination? Only you know what you want to cover. And, to some level, you can control the flow of the conversation, but you need to make sure you know where you want it to go. It's easy to get sidetracked in conversations with new people.

If it's helpful to create this in a written document, then do that, even if it's bullet points to remind you of specific topics. You can share as the meeting starts that you want to make sure you cover topics X, Y, and Z. When you meet with people, they generally want the conversation to be beneficial because they often don't have time to meet again soon. Maybe they can follow up with an email or two, but their time is generally limited, like yours.

Limit the Time You Talk about Your Kids

Do not *only* talk about kids, especially to fellow parents. As moms, we can talk all day about our kids — how amazing they are, our struggles as parents, and even the fun things we're doing as a family. Cover the topic of kids and family stuff and move on. As much as you might want to talk about a challenge or solve someone else's challenge with something related to kids, that is not the purpose of the conversation.

Guide the Conversation

As the initiator of the conversation, it's your role to manage and guide the conversation. It's important to not abruptly change the conversation, because no one likes to be cut off and you don't want that to set the stage for the conversation. Figure out an easy, natural transition from the topic of kids to other areas. For example, talk about kids for a few minutes, which does require you keep an eye on time. Then, as a transition, ask how the other parent keeps all the balls in the air. Ask about his or her time management or tips and tools for keeping everything on track. It will make the transition to talking about the professional side of things easier. You can figure out what works transition-wise for you and seems natural. And practice, if you need to, so that it's not awkward or forced.

Don't do All the Talking

Are you excited and passionate about the topic you're talking about? That is great, but it might also be a hindrance. You don't want to do all the talking during this conversation. Articulate what you're looking for in a two- to five-minute elevator pitch. Practice your pitch at home or even in the car when you don't have kids with you. You want your pitch to be natural and easily flow off your tongue.

Another point to consider is your communication style. Do you talk a lot? I'm a talker and I know it. In the end, I want to network, not have the other person write my biography. I am aware of how much I talk and you might need to be as well. You want to share, but make your sharing concise and purposeful.

Alternatively, what happens if you're meeting someone new and you're not very outgoing? You need to show a level of enthusiasm and confidence during your interaction. Again, practice, practice, practice. Make sure you practice aloud and not only in your head. You might see places where you naturally get tripped up as you explain what you've been working on and what you want moving forward.

While networking might seem like a daunting task, it's a chance to get to know people. These new connections might introduce you to a new opportunity. Treat the interaction less as a line item on the to-do list and more as a new person who you connect with. These new people can potentially be in your life for years to come or they might be a gatekeeper to someone amazing. Enjoy it!

Follow Up

This is the part that I think people forget. We use the advice from our networking interactions and we move on. Circle back to the person you have just networked with. Make sure you take care of any next steps as quickly as you can after you meet. If you say you're going to send something to the person who you've been networking with, do it. You might have mentioned an article or a resource you use; email it with any pertinent information. Connect the dots so the person understands how this relates to your recent conversation. For example, "Jane, I mentioned that I use a resource for my research on X topic. Since you're looking into that topic, you might find the tool I use helpful."

If you've met with someone and want to leave an impression, send a note via email or, better yet, a handwritten note (if you know the person's address). It can be a simple thank you for their time or share a tidbit you found incredibly helpful or enlightening from your conversation.

And keep in touch with this person over time, so that if you do reach out again, there won't be a long lag between communications. You can send articles that relate to his or her business or project, or resources or press releases on something they're involved with. Send them whenever you find them to keep a connection alive. Don't send too much though, since that can be a bit overwhelming on the receiving end. You're looking to keep the connection alive over time.

Return the Favor

While some people might network with you and introduce you to others they know as an act of kindness, some may want something in return. Or you might want to offer something, but what? Ask what that person needs. What is she working on that you might be able to help with? You might have a skill that is missing on her team or maybe you know someone who could be a good resource. If you can't help with a particular topic or area, do you know someone who can? If not, perhaps this isn't the best use of your skills and offer something that still might help solve that challenge. Or ask if you can be helpful in another area, where you can provide some expertise or connections. See if they know someone who needs help with something or an introduction to the industry you work in (e.g., daughter, niece, neighbor's child, etc.).

Networking Playdates

I'm including a concept in this chapter that has slightly different parameters, but it's still a networking where you are type of opportunity. Instead of asking another mom you'd like to network with to take time away from her kids and her work stuff, how about you both take time *with* kids to network? Pick a fun spot for kids — playground, park, splash pad, whatever works. Somewhere the kids are generally safe and can play together. The kids are entertained and likely having fun with limited effort from moms and moms get to network. Win-win for all participants. It's also great to do during summer and winter breaks when parents are trying to figure out what to do with kids.

The ways to get the most out of it are a bit different than usual networking interactions, so here are some things to consider.

- If your kids are the about same age, great. If not, do your kids play with kids who aren't their own age? Choose a good spot for kids of a variety of ages or skip the networking playdate if your kids won't play with kids who aren't their age.

- You want a location that all the kids find fun without mom's constant nudging and attention. For example, don't take infants who can barely walk to a playground designed for kindergarteners or that mom will constantly be distracted by her young child's safety.

- Make sure your kids aren't tired or hungry and try to avoid times when this will be the case (e.g., skip afternoon get-togethers if your kids need a nap). You know what works and what doesn't for your child and make sure you know what works and doesn't for the other kids involved.

- Take care of logistics and know the basics of the location, if you're the one who suggested the location. What time does the place open and/or close? Where are the restrooms? Is the area shaded? If not, bring sunblock for all the kids. Is there going to be loud music playing? Is it fenced in or is it attached to an area where kids can easily get lost or wander off? Do you need to meet in the front if it's large or is there an easy meeting place? You get the idea. As the initiator of the playdate and probably the location as well, know what you're getting into.

- If you are receiving all the benefit for this networking inter-action, pay for whatever your networking partner and her children get or any fees associated with the location. Pay for a drink, treat for the kids, etc. It's a small expense in comparison to what you're getting. Consider it business etiquette.

- If the place you're going doesn't serve food and beverages, take snacks that have widespread appeal for kids, which are acceptable to other moms (e.g., cut up fruit and maybe some-thing like animal crackers that most kids love), and avoid the unusual things your kids love. It seems like anytime kids start playing, one says "I'm hungry" and they all nod their heads, even when they've *just* eaten. The idea is to take something to give to *all* the kids, not only yours, whenever they do get hun-gry. Because they will.

- And, finally, enjoy yourself and don't stress too much. You're being productive and your kids are occupied, most likely hav-ing fun.

In summary:

- Take advantage of the built-in networks you have around you, both personal and professional.
- Be specific with your networking approach and strategy.
- Do your homework before you meet.
- Know what points you want to cover to guide the conversa-tion.
- Make sure you follow up.
- Return the favor whenever you can.
- Limit your time to talk about kids and know how to transition.
- Consider networking playdates with other moms.

CHAPTER 15:

SAHMS CAN SET THEMSELVES UP FOR SUCCESS AS A PPWM

THIS BOOK IS LARGELY designed for moms who currently work full time and are interested in reducing their schedule, so they can take that time and use it for personal, usually family-related, needs. There is no question that going back to work after a time away, even as little as a year or two, makes everything harder. That said, there are a few moms in the interviews who did go back to work after stepping away from their career and I know plenty of moms are in their shoes. Setting yourself up for success as a PPWM looks a bit different for a SAHM and I've included additional pieces of advice specifically geared towards the SAHM looking to reenter the workforce.

Professional Part-time Roles and Lifestyles

When a SAHM in Connecticut went back to work after being at home for eleven years, she found an industry and role that didn't require she make huge changes in her lifestyle. She found a job not too far from home in media sales, with hours that work for her family. With three kids involved in several activities, she needed to be able to pick them up from school, head to activities, and then head home. And flexibility already built in was a must.

When I asked her advice, her biggest tip was to find a role that fits your lifestyle instead of fitting your lifestyle into a new role. She admits this changes from person to person, so it takes some soul searching to figure out what works for your situation. It might also take a discussion with your significant other or even someone else who is close to the situation like a caregiver. The goal is to make sure everyone is on the same page and supportive.

And an added layer of complexity is that the role you left to have kids might not be the type of role that you want now. And that might require you to do some soul searching on what you're looking for and what you want to do. It will help to talk to people about roles related to what you did before or related to a new area of interest to get the scoop from a person instead of a job description on a website.

Try to find someone in the field and especially in the role who you can shadow to give you an in-person idea of what the job (and company) is like. This is an exceedingly productive way to gain perspective that will help with deciding if this is the right role for you, if you can find a person willing to let you shadow him or her.

What do You Want to Do?

You know you want to go back to work, but you're not exactly sure what you want to do. Let's start with what you did before. Did you enjoy it or was motherhood the perfect time to stop doing that work? If you enjoyed it, maybe it's a good idea to go back into that industry, even if you're not quite sure of the role yet. If it wasn't really the best industry or role for you, were there elements you enjoyed or is that role and industry something you will leave in the past?

Another area to consider is your volunteer roles. What have you enjoyed in your volunteering? Are there topics or specific roles that you've become passionate about that you'd like to explore professionally? What skills have you picked up that you are good at that open up a new industry where you can apply your skills? Figure out how to build on these areas. Not sure what they might translate into? Grab a friend or a group of friends and brainstorm. It's often helpful to bounce ideas around with someone else, instead of figuring it out alone. And it's really helpful to talk to someone who has worked before or currently works in that industry or role, who understands your skill set, whether through volunteering or from before you became a SAHM.

Skills Assessment

Now that you're looking for roles that fit your needs, do you have the right skills for the industry or role you're interested in? If you haven't worked in a few years or more, you want to make sure your skills are on par with expectations in the industry. This is even more important if you're trying to pivot into a new industry.

Not sure if you're still on your game? Start with looking at online profiles to see how they describe their skills and their roles. Look at job descriptions that seem to describe what you want to do, even if you're not quite to the point of doing a job search. How do your own skills stack up against others and what gaps exist? Have conversations with people you know in the industry. Ask about the skills they expect from those at their same level or levels below. If you don't know someone right now in the industry, use your network to get to the right people.

Are there specific skills needed to even be considered for a position or tools commonly used that might not have been used even a few years ago when you transitioned to be a SAHM? If so and if you've been keeping everything up to date in relation to your skill set, then you're set.

Look for resources for moms reentering the workforce on the Recommended Resources tab of www.mompowerment.com.

Updating or Upgrading Skills

If your skills aren't up to date, what can you do to update them? An initial step is to start reading industry publications, expert blogs, websites, or well-respected books. That might help you figure out where to focus your attention moving forward. Once you're more able to devote time, look for classes in your area and online. Check colleges or universities nearby for informal and enrichment classes. See what is offered by a nearby community college. Depending on the industry, there could even be courses offered through the local chamber of commerce or at low-cost workshops or conferences in your area. There might even be courses specifically for moms wanting to reenter the workforce near you, so do an online search for what's available in your area.

In addition to courses offered in person, there are all sorts of options online. Do the research to understand who the online experts are on a topic or in a field. See who is publishing articles in the industry publications or who's being quoted. Maybe they are speaking at events. Or simply ask people you know in the industry who is respected as an expert online on a topic. That way you can see if those experts offer courses or maybe endorse a course or workshop offered by someone else. Some online experts offer free webinars to introduce you to a topic. Maybe consider doing more than one free or introductory course before signing up for something that requires a fee or an investment. These initial or introductory courses can help you figure out what you don't know, so that you can start building a roadmap with next steps and a timeline for learning a new skill.

It's helpful to consider updating skills before you start your official job search. You might need time to understand what's out there, when the courses are offered, and complete an application process for courses, if that applies. From a cost perspective, sometimes these types of classes can be costly and you will want to build the cost into your budget.

Resume and Online Profile

When was the last time you updated your resume? It's helpful to keep your resume updated as time passes instead of trying to figure things out when you're ready to get back into the workforce. If you haven't updated it over time, dig in one day when kids aren't around and make a first pass at an update. It doesn't have to be perfect. More than anything, you need a starting point. Take smaller chunks after that initial pass and work on specific areas at a time or even specific roles.

Make sure to have an online professional profile on a provider like LinkedIn. If it's been a while since you've been in the workforce, this might be new to you. Don't let it overwhelm you. Break things down into more reasonable chunks, instead of trying to perfect an online profile overnight.

Start by filling out what you did before kids. You don't want this to be an online resume, but start with that and build on it. Talk about the important aspects of what you did and not simply a detailed job description. Start connecting to people you know from your past roles. Ask people you have worked with to endorse your skills or to give you a testimonial or recommendation, so that other people can see this and understand your skill set.

One key theme you will want throughout your resume and online profile is a pattern of excellence in all that you do. Take time upfront to identify what projects and initiatives you have led and their outcomes. This exercise can extend to volunteer work you've done recently if you've been out of work (see next section). Highlight these accomplishments and the results in both your resume and online profile to demonstrate that you've always done excellent work and, when given the opportunity, will continue to do so.

If you do find it overwhelming, there are individuals and companies that provide this service and they can help you get your online profile and resume more geared toward specific industries or roles. I link to a few of these resources on www.mompowerment.com.

The Career Benefit of Volunteering

You might be wondering how to fill a resume when you haven't worked for the last few or ten years. In my experience, many SAHMs do quite a bit of volunteering. Maybe you volunteer at your child's school or in an organization related to something you're passionate about.

What do you do in that role? Sit down and think about what you do or did as a volunteer. It's not as simple as a single line on your resume and online profile. And, honestly, it shouldn't be. Take advantage of the skills you built in volunteering and help others understand your new skills or previous skills that you've built on.

Are you in charge of fundraising and you head up the efforts to raise tens of thousands of dollars? Maybe you managed other volunteers or a whole team? Were you a committee chair, managing projects and a small group of volunteers with specific tasks to complete by a deadline? These volunteer roles speak to management, fundraising, project management, and leadership skills, which are highly sought after in the workforce. Talk about these roles and skills like you would a position in the workforce on your resume and online profiles.

Think about the business elements of your volunteer roles and not only as a thing you do at your child's school. If you're struggling with how to describe what you do or can't quite see the importance, ask a friend for help. Describe what you do to a friend and record yourself on your phone to hear the specific words you use. Or even ask the school or leadership of the organization about why they have the role. Ask specifically about the importance of your role or your team. You want to understand the end benefit because that is part of what should be on your resume and online profile. Also, get administration you worked with or strategic leads at the organization, such as the director of the school or executive director of the organization, to endorse your skills online and provide a reference.

Volunteering and Job Hunting

Some moms who were SAHMs found a job through their volunteering. A mom who works part time in education moved to a new city for her husband's job. She wasn't really sure about her future career efforts, so she got really involved in her children's school. She chaired a major event for the school and had no idea that it would lead to a job. She was three weeks away from having her second child when the event happened and decided to take about a year off before returning to work. And, based on the amazing job she did with the event and changes that happened at the school, they approached her to take on a position at the school. When she shared that she was interested in a part-time role, the school adjusted their needs to match hers. The opportunity probably wouldn't have happened without her volunteer role.

Maintaining and Growing Your Network

Networking is integral for SAHMs looking to get back into the workforce. Think about it: your network understands your skills, expertise, drive, work style, etc. As an Atlanta-based lawyer, who works fewer than forty hours a week, put it, "Your reputation and skills are already known by your network."

Keeping in contact with them and showing how you're still engaged with elements of your career can go far. A nonprofit fundraising consultant, who works ten to twenty hours per week, in the New York City Tri-State Area, shared that her boss knows her work product and has faith that she'll get everything done because she worked for him previously. Instead of hiring someone new when he needed help, he brought her on to his new team because she had been an integral member of his team previously.

In addition to talking to people in person, stay engaged with your online network. Keep your online professional profile up-to-date and reach out to your online network periodically. Ask what they're working on. Send them articles that you read about their companies, clients, industries, etc. Show that you're still engaged with elements of your career, even if you're not career-focused at that moment.

If you're volunteering, share what you're involved with and the roles, especially leadership roles that you've taken on. Talk about the results that your volunteer roles are making in the organization and in the community.

Part time as a Springboard to a Full-time Role

When a mom who had been a SAHM for twelve years went back into the workforce, she realized that she couldn't go into a full-time role and be the mom she wanted to be, at least not initially. Her suggestion is for SAHMs, who have been home for several years, to get their feet wet in a part-time capacity before transitioning into a full-time role. And she suggests that SAHMs "prepare for a culture shock when they head back into the workforce." It's a big shift to go from generally working full time, to becoming a SAHM, to joining the workforce again, whether in a part-time or full-time capacity.

Returnship Opportunity

An idea that is gaining traction is for moms to do internships or "returnships" as they have been called. See if you can shadow someone or try to get an internship for a short period (e.g., six months or fewer). In the best-case scenario, you should be paid for your time. Some large, well-known companies are doing these as a paid opportunity, including for career switchers. If you're interested in a company that doesn't offer a returnship, you might even consider offering to do the work for free for a few months (e.g., two or three) to truly understand what the role takes and to update your skills, especially if it's a company you're interested in or if you're looking to do a career transition.

Imagine the statement you make that you took the initiative to seek out an internship (or worked for free to learn about a new industry, role, company, etc.). Make sure to get a recommendation, which ideally is both on your online profile and a reference that you can include for a job interview. You want to ask before you complete your time at the company for that online reference and confirm their willingness to be a reference.

Building Your Work Confidence

You've been out of the workforce for a few months, a few years, or more than a decade. Moms who were out of the workforce for a period said it was important to walk away from negative thoughts if you're feeling less confident in your skills and relevancy.

You chose to leave your career to dedicate yourself full time to your family. That was the right choice for you and your family in that moment. You're now ready to start focusing more on your career and you might need to mentally prepare for that.

Don't worry about the gap on your resume. Be confident in explaining that you chose to take time off and that you're ready to get back into a game professionally. Talk about why now is the right time. Maybe there is something you're excited about in the industry. Maybe you learned a new skill through volunteering and you can't wait to use it professionally. Articulate whatever is drawing you back to work. And let being a SAHM be a part of your story, as this new chapter is a continuation of your professional story. Doing the exercise related to finding your patterns of excellence mentioned in the Resume and Online Profile sections of this chapter can help to build that confidence.

Practice talking about your background, what is drawing you back to work, and what skills you have. You probably haven't had to do this for a while. Practice in the car when your kids aren't around or while doing household chores. Be confident in what you bring to the table and why now is the right time and share that when networking and interviewing for a job.

In summary:

- SAHMs interested in becoming PPWMs have additional steps they should take as they prepare for and begin their job search.
- It's important to stay engaged with your network, even if you don't plan on reentering the workforce any time soon.
- Moms who have been out of the workforce for an extended time must do a skills assessment before starting the job search.
- Once a skills assessment is complete, SAHMs should consider ways to learn new skills.
- SAHMs should update their resume and online profile before it's necessary for a job search.
- Volunteering can be a resume builder, so understand and articulate the business side of those volunteer roles.
- Before beginning the job search, SAHMs can consider shorter work projects, such as internships, to update or learn new skills and to understand new roles or industries.
- Build your confidence as you start networking and interviewing.

PART IV:
SKILLS, TOOLS, AND SYSTEMS THAT
ENABLE SUCCESS FOR PPWMS

CASE STUDY: When You Have a Demanding Career and Want Balance

This OBGYN is one of two doctors in a job share in a smaller practice with seven other full-time doctors. After working full-time as an OBGYN for five years, she found herself in the perfect storm for quitting her job. She was married with two kids, one of whom wasn't even a year old, and she was helping with a family health issue.

She walked away from medicine for eighteen months to become a SAHM. The OBGYN has been working part time in a job share scenario for about eleven years, working about thirty to forty hours per week in comparison to sixty or more hours per week for full-time OBGYNs. Planning, sometimes months in advance, is largely how the two job share partners work well. They both get one consistent day off each week and plan in two-week periods to make sure they know what's coming up.

This OBGYN gets work-life balance in her part-time situation. She even has one-on-one time with each of her three children. And she has time with her husband. She's not sure she could manage all of that working full time in a specialty within the medical field, which is emotionally demanding and time-sensitive. And, since the OBGYN knows she has time with her family and time for her patients, she is present in whichever situation she's in.

Her advice for anyone interested in working part time:

- *Women have choices.* Whether career-related or in their personal lives, women have choices. Don't feel pressured to go down your career path and then turn your attention to your personal life.

- *Understand what help you need.* Part of what makes her situation work is that she has a nanny. She shares that having that outside help is integral to everything working. Acknowledge your limitations and areas you don't want to do and get the help you need and want.

- *Don't compare your situation to others.* You don't know what goes on behind their closed doors, so you don't really understand anyone's story.

- *Do what you love.* You have limited time to work each day, so make sure to love what you do with the time constraints you have.

CHAPTER 16:

PRODUCTIVITY, TIME MANAGEMENT AND STAYING ON TASK

THE CONCEPTS OF PRODUCTIVITY, time management, and staying on task are closely related. Productivity is making the most of your time. Time management is being efficient with the time you have. Once you set aside the time and start working, you need to stay on task. For example, I have many things to accomplish in one day. I've set aside two hours to get three blog posts done. Each one will take thirty minutes plus ten minutes to revise, if I'm being efficient and productive with my time. To actually be productive and make the most of the time, I must stay on task, which means no social media or checking email. I need all three — productivity, time management, and staying on task — to get those three blog posts written, revised, and ready to go.

Productivity

Those of you who watched my talk from TEDxSMU Women know that productivity is one of my hot buttons. I think there are flaws in how companies look at productivity or maybe I should describe it as there is a lack of measuring employees based on productivity.

The current eight-hour workday commonly used in the United States today was put in place by two large printing firms in 1906.[1] And a federal law, the Adamson Act, was passed by Congress in 1916 to create an eight-hour workday for railroad workers.[2] Today's standard forty-hour work week is commonly linked back to Henry Ford since he instituted this schedule in his factories in 1926 and helped popularize this approach.[3]

It's almost 100 years later and we make and do all sorts of new things, but we still use that forty-hour work week as the standard for how we measure people, not their productivity. Essentially, we measure people on hours – at least forty for most salaried employees. Why do we treat all employees the same each day, measuring the number of hours they have worked? And how is it that productivity doesn't play into the daily measurement?

A World Economic Forum study show that employees stop being productive at about twenty-five hours per week.[4] People in roles that require a lot of brain power might have even less productivity time.[5]

The other time is unproductive, but employees are still at the office. If you work for someone else, you know what I mean when I say the way you're usually measured is hours working. For things like promotions or bonuses, maybe productivity and contribution come into play. Why isn't productivity used for measuring employees daily? We could reward employees for being more productive instead of requiring them to work for eight or more hours each day.

If you're an employee, you might be thinking, "My manager measures employees by their productivity." Here is the test to see if that is true. You go to your manager at 3 p.m. a few days in a row and let him or her know that you're done with your work goals for the day. This isn't a special day in that you didn't say you needed to leave by 3 p.m. for something. You're simply being more productive with your time. Does he or she let you leave because you've completed what is necessary for the day? Or does your manager give you more work? If it's the latter, your manager and employer probably aren't measuring employees based on their productivity.

If your employer doesn't look at productivity, they're the norm.

Things have changed since that forty-hour work week was put in place, so maybe it's time to start thinking differently so that we keep great employees engaged. Maybe we need to reflect employees' level of productivity and efficiency, not only hours at work. We shouldn't keep people at the office (or simply working if they work from home) because they have to complete at least eight hours of work each day, without question. We can reward employees for finishing their tasks in fewer than eight hours when they're proven they can reach their daily, weekly, or monthly goals.

Productivity-focused Companies

Some companies have started using productivity to manage their employees.[6] In the case of Tower Paddle Boards, a small stand up paddle board business based out of San Diego, California, the owner, Stephen Aarstol, wasn't sure what would happen to productivity when he reduced the work week to twenty-five hours during a three-month test. He argued, "At the same time that people have the ability to be massively more productive, they also now have the ability to massively waste time."[7] Aarstol wrote an article in *Fast Company* and shared that more than a year later, the five-hour workday is still the company's approach, and revenue is continuing its upward trend.[8]

And, when you think about it, that probably allows for a reduction in some operational costs. If people aren't spending as much time together, they probably don't need as much space, which cuts down both on the necessary real estate and the energy used at an office.

I recognize that there are some roles and even whole industries that won't really be productivity-focused. For example, we need people to care for patients around the clock at hospitals and elder care facilities. I would argue, though, that even some roles within those facilities could be productivity-based, such as accounting, marketing, and other operational or management roles.

Do you Need to Change Your Own Approach to Productivity?

When a mom decides she wants to work part time, she might discover she needs to change how she works to complete all her tasks in a shorter period. I discuss aspects of productivity based on my own experience and that of moms I interviewed. These are a few approaches that work, but there are others out there.

It's helpful to understand how you're most productive, so I highly recommend doing some research and trying a few options out to see what works best for you. There are all sorts of ways to be more efficient with your time, once you know what you're spending time on.

Figure Out your Productivity Rhythms

Each person is unique in his or her productivity. Figure out your most productive time, since you're at your peak performance then. Understand your least productive times and consider limiting the amount of work you do at that point of your day. Seems simple, but it takes you understanding your own rhythms and then using that knowledge to help you with your time management and productivity.

It happens I am at my most productive in the morning and for a few hours in the evening. Early afternoon is when I have my natural lull. I set up my calendar with these elements in mind. For example, I work as much as possible in the morning when I'm at my best. I volunteer mid-day or in the afternoon at our boys' schools or I will schedule non-essential calls (e.g., calls that aren't client-related or don't have direct impact on my business). I might read a bit of a business book or do dinner prep once we get home after school and the boys are doing quiet time. The idea is early to mid-afternoon isn't active work time. And I can re-engage, if necessary, on business stuff, once the boys are asleep.

See what works in your situation and don't be afraid to experiment. It might take a few tries to figure out your best time to work or maybe the best time to work on different elements of your job or to-do list (e.g., writing in the morning versus calls after lunch).

Work on Top Priorities First

It feels good to cross a bunch of things off your to do list throughout the day. If you take that approach, will you spend enough time on your most important tasks? Laura Vanderkam, an expert on time management and productivity and author of *I Know How She Does It and What the Most Successful People Do Before Breakfast*, suggests that instead of checking off a bunch of things first, focus initially on priorities and then sprinkle in the rest.[9]

I do major client work and writing as soon as I get back from dropping off my boys at school. Even though it feels good to check a bunch of boxes, it's best to be at my freshest for my priorities, instead of working on my sometimes incredibly long to-do list.

Batching or Blocks of Time

At the office, you need both time to work to get things done and time to engage with your clients and team. Boundaries help you divide up that time effectively. Essentially, you establish blocks of time to do different types of tasks. This can also be referred to as batching.

Several moms mentioned batching, which is how I work as well. It's the idea that combining similar tasks makes you more efficient than trying to switch back and forth between different kinds of tasks. When it's writing time, I write several blog posts, guest blog posts, etc. in one block of time or I research for different projects in one block since I'm already in that mode.

To be at my most efficient, I combine blocks of time with the Pomodoro technique, where I work twenty-five minutes and then do something else for five minutes, and then work twenty-five minutes and do something else for five minutes, and so on. After several of these intervals, I take a longer break.[10]

I have done this approach long enough so that I naturally stop after about twenty-five minutes. Since that's not the case with most moms who are starting to use this productivity method, use a timer or your calendar reminders. That way you have physical reminders that it's time to let your mind take a break and then you can get back to your work. And you can still use those five minutes for things related to your business or for personal things you need to do.

Time Management

Tracking Time

Part of being more efficient with your time is understanding how you're spending your time. Laura Vanderkam suggests having a better understanding of how you spend your time over the course of a week: "If you want to lose weight, you keep a food diary. If you want to get out of debt, you record your spending. Likewise, if you want to use your time better, you should keep track of your time."[11]

This is a helpful first step in understanding where your time currently goes before trying to figure out where it can go. And it allows you to understand how much time you're using for your various tasks, whether on the professional or personal side. Once you track this and get a good idea of your normal schedule (e.g., don't track during the weekend or holidays), you can start assessing your schedule and what areas you might want to change.[12]

Work During Naptime

An astrophysicist researcher at a university in Austin, Texas, shared that when her kids were young, she made sure to work during naptime. She described it as the naptime hustle. For moms who work from home, this is can be an integral element of time management.

It's helpful to have a plan for what you can get done during naptime. Prepare for it, so that you can be most efficient and productive during the time. Have your prioritized list ready. I use the time to work and won't usually schedule phone calls during naptime in case our younger son doesn't nap or naps for a short time. When he naps it's an extra hour and I can get stuff done.

If you have a newborn or young infant, consider planning for naptime differently since sleep times can be inconsistent initially. Use small increments of time to be productive. Business expert Dana Malstaff suggests breaking the day down into ten or fifteen minute increments and looks at what she can do from her phone, such as read a relevant article or respond to an email from a team member or client. The little pockets of time can keep you, your team, and your clients moving toward bigger goals.[13]

If you notice that naptime is longer over several days, then you can check off more tasks on your to do list. As the naps get longer, break things down into larger chunks and tackle those bigger projects. Always remember to have your smaller goals prioritized, so you can get to it as soon as the clock (so to speak) starts.[14]

Focus

The third part of this trio is the ability to stay on task or focus. It's incredibly important and the other two don't happen without focus.

Have Specific Goals for the Day

We all have our goals for our projects, but what about your daily goals? To be more efficient on a daily basis, I started creating daily goals so that I know exactly what I have to do each day to build up to my bigger goals. I try to have three to five things that I'm trying to achieve for the day. This requires me breaking down a bigger goal into bite-sized chunks. Some of these things might be something small like registering my child for a school activity, but there is a deadline and a benefit to taking a bit of time to get it done. For work, I might specifically spend one hour researching a specific slice of a topic for a client project. This approach of three to five smaller goals keeps me on task.

If you want to try to break down your goals, you might assign a time period to go along with working on each goal. An event planner and business coach in Chicago, who works about forty hours a week, suggests "scheduling out your work day in whatever increments [make sense] for you." Her suggestions were fifteen- and thirty-minute segments. And you can align those increments with your goals, so you prioritize. This might help with keeping you on track instead of getting sidetracked by things like social media.

Meal Preparation

Productivity isn't only for your professional tasks. You can improve productivity with your parental or household duties as well. One of the areas most mentioned by moms from their personal lives in interviews was meal preparation. For most of the moms I interviewed, they are the person in charge of household duties on top of being the default parent, which means having dinner on the table falls squarely on their shoulder. There were a few moms who shared they don't cook and that is a responsibility of their significant other, but these were few. (If your significant other does the cooking —and does a good job — you have found a keeper, ladies.)

How can you make meal prep easier? Moms I interviewed shared their tips and I also include my own:

Being More Efficient with your Time During Meal Prep

- Use a slow cooker, especially on nights when there are evening activities or when mom is away from home all day.
- Cook all or most meals on the weekend and freeze whatever won't be eaten in the next two to three days and then thaw out meals for the end of the week.

- Make enough food for two meals, so that you're only actively cooking three or four nights a week.
- If your family doesn't like having the same meal two nights in a row, have enough entrée for two nights and change the sides (e.g., rice and zucchini one night, and butter noodles and peas another). It takes less time to make the sides than to make two totally different main courses.
- Freeze a meal for another night. We often make enough for three nights. Two consecutive nights we change the sides and we freeze the final portion for another night, when I won't have time to prep a meal from scratch.
- Take time to look at labels to find healthy frozen options you don't mind having in a pinch.

Applying Planning to the Meal Prep Process

- Plan meals for the week so that you visit the grocery store only once each week for all ingredients and replace staple items.
- Consider an online service that either delivers groceries on your list or that sends all the ingredients portioned out, so that all you have to do is prepare it.
- Using consistent themes each day or two days of the week (e.g., taco day(s) versus rice bowl day(s)). Hint: Use the same entrée for two different themes. For example, chicken tacos one day and chicken and rice bowl the next.

Meal Prep Short Cuts

- Making breakfast for dinner is something we do about once every few weeks. It can be pancakes, eggs, oatmeal, or whatever is easy to make that your family loves.
- Wash fruit and veggies and even chop whatever needs to be chopped when it first comes home from the grocery store. It can save time later.

- Wash all the fruits and vegetables for the day in the morning if you're prepping lunches for school.

Prepping the Night Before

A tip that I heard in many interviews also happens to be something I do as well. Make sure you use the night before to help with your overall productivity.

Work Preparation

When it comes to work, on the night before look at what you want to do the following day, especially in the morning. Set up the three to five goals and decide the most important things on your list. Do anything that might be able to help you get your results the next day. For example, look strategically at how your day naturally maps out with projects, calls, meetings, etc. and plan your day. Put bullet points together for something you're writing. Organize any research you've done so that you can hit the ground running with the project instead of wading through the research first.

If you're heading to a meeting, print out anything you need to physically take and have copies ready. Or put the presentation in a folder you can easily find on a USB drive or email it to yourself. You never know what the morning might look like, especially with kids. All that time you thought you might have in the morning might be spent cleaning up a massive spill or a blow-out. You might have to change your black slacks because your sweet toddler hugged you when his hands were covered in cream cheese from his toasted bagel. Or technology might not work, because it seems like that's what happens when you need technology to be your friend. I know you've experienced the moments I'm talking about if you're a mom. Take care of it the night before and avoid stress in the morning.

Getting Bags Ready

There are personal things you can do at night to help you get your morning going faster. Put your laptop and/or notebooks in your work bag. Get backpacks and baby bags ready with things like labeled diapers and snacks that don't require refrigeration. Make sure you label anything that needs to be labeled (e.g., food containers), so that you don't have to do that in the morning after checking. (You can get a link to the specific labels I use for everything from water bottles to clothing on www.mompowerment.com under Recommended Resources.) Once the bags are ready to go the evening before, put them by the door.

Put Things in a Consistent Spot

Our car keys hang on a special hook by the front door. The boys' shoes are always in the mudroom. I don't have time to look for shoes every morning for ten minutes. Have a place for everything, especially the things you use daily. It simply makes them easier to find, so that takes less effort.

Have things ready for the next step. For example, put out lunch boxes with containers on the counter, so you know exactly where they are and won't have to go find them. I put a fun napkin in our young son's lunchbox, ready to go. It's a small touch that our older son loves and it's easy, especially when I do it the night before.

Lunch Preparation

If you're still making lunch for your kids, which is my situation, think about what you can prepare the night before. A few moms I interviewed suggested making the entire lunch the night before. I don't make sandwiches the night before, but I do some prep such as washing fruit or putting things that don't need refrigeration in the lunchbox. I'm also consistent with what I call my "formula" for the boys' lunch. It generally consists of a sandwich, two to three kinds of fruit, and, for our older son, some sort of treat. Putting the treat in the lunch the night before takes care of one step and also keeps me from forgetting it.

Clothing Choices

Have everyone in the house pick out clothes and lay them out the night before. Both of our young boys now have opinions on what they wear, so it's their choice. I provide input if necessary (e.g., it's picture day or it's going to be 100 degrees, so no long sleeve shirts). It also limits the number of challenges or discussions in the morning and can decrease tears.

A therapist in Alabama, who works ten to thirty-five hours a week, schedules what she'll wear for the month, so that she uses no mental energy on this aspect of her life. If you know your schedule weeks in advance or even for the week, you can use this approach to plan your wardrobe for long periods instead of daily.

I have friends who have essentially the same general outfit, but an element changes. They have the same tops, bottoms, and accessories in different colors. It's consistent and requires little mental energy to figure things out, especially if all the items generally color coordinate. You know it will look good on you and you know it all goes together, so it's a low-stress wardrobe.

To-Do List versus Did List

Anyone who knows me well, knows I love my to-do lists. I keep a single list of everything that needs to be done in both professional and personal areas. My thought is that I'm the one doing it all, so I keep everything on one list broken out into different categories.

What most people don't know is I also have a "did" list, which I highly recommend. In my case, it's the same list as my to-do list.

I use my notebook for my to-do list, so my did list is what's been checked off. It helps me see what I've accomplished in a day or week. And that is something that keeps me motivated. Sometimes, you need to see how far you've come on projects or see your productive moments. If you do online to-do lists, you can mark through lists as well instead of deleting a completed task. Once you're ready for a new list, keep a separate place to track accomplishments you want to highlight over time.

Adjust as Necessary

A mom, who works about twenty-eight hours per week in an operations role at an organization that does social work, shared that initially her day off was Monday. She realized she had to change things. She felt disconnected professionally when she got into the office on Tuesday after being away or three consecutive days. It took a lot more effort to re-engage and focus on work. She switched her day off to Thursday and it's helped keep her engaged and still enables her to take a full day off.

An Atlanta-based business meeting consultant who works five to twenty hours per week shared that figuring out a schedule was her biggest challenge. She explained that it took a while to get her rhythm and balance right. She found her rhythm once both her girls were on same schedule, which happened when her younger daughter went to preschool.

Essentially, for some moms, they need small adjustments and then they hit their stride. For other moms, it took a large shift like taking a different day off. And for some moms, it takes time to get into your rhythm. Give yourself time and the permission to adjust so that you hit your productivity stride.

If you have an employer, build in an adjustment phase. Or review the situation after an agreed-upon period (e.g., three months) to see what adjustments need to be made, whether from your end or your manager's. When you do this, make sure not to start adjusting too soon. I mention three months because it can take ninety days to get into a groove for any job. If you haven't even had time to get into a rhythm after reducing hours, how can you start making adjustments?

That said, if you immediately notice things aren't working, talk to your manager or team about changing things up. And be open to your manager or team talking to you about things that need to be fixed quickly. If you don't agree, table the discussion for the agreed-upon timing.

How Breathing Space Helps with Productivity

One of the concepts that really struck a chord with me in the interviews was about the idea of "breathing space." A doctor of internal medicine in Austin, Texas, who works fewer than thirty hours a week, shared how "breathing space" in her life was one of the benefits of working part time.

What is breathing space? For me, it's a pause that I take in my day. I might use it to assess the moment and figure out next steps. I take breathing space to confront and combat the feeling of overwhelm when my to-do list seems to be as long as my arm and only getting longer. That pause can really help me think through challenges. It can also help me understand what I need in that moment and moving forward.

We're all busy. Our lives pull us in all different directions every day. Some days we have it together and some days we barely hold on. We go from one thing to another to keep all the plates spinning at the same time.

Moms describe taking calls in the car while waiting in the pick-up line in efforts to use every hour of the day and be incredibly productive. I am a proponent of being your most efficient and productive when you work. When we do that though, we don't get a moment of transition and we lose the breathing space we might need. We go from professional to mom with no buffer between the two. I do this every school day. Even though my husband's commute is only fifteen to twenty minutes, that still allows him to have a transition time from professional to dad and husband.

Include time in your day and week, as an element of your productivity, to assess and address your needs. Maybe intentionally having more breathing space can help with having more have-it-together moments and fewer barely-holding-on times.

Consider the visual version of this concept. In design, the visual aspect is as much the stuff you want to look at as it is the white space around that stuff. You need the two to be balanced or your eye doesn't know where to look. It's too busy and is a sensory overload without focus.

It's the same idea with the breathing space – the downtime – that your brain needs to make the rest of the time more productive and efficient. We simply can't be at our highest productivity 100 percent of the time, even though we might think we can. And, realize it might be different for each person. Some moms use exercise to help them take a pause in their day. Other moms might meditate. Other moms still might practice self-care.

In my case, without breathing space, the Mompowerment book probably wouldn't exist. If I simply kept working with clients in my consulting business and didn't look around to think about the lack of stories about PPWMs, I wouldn't have realized the stories aren't really out there. I wouldn't have thought about bringing the stories together in a book, creating a community, and empowering moms to think differently about their career approach.

In summary:

- Productivity is incredibly important to PPWMs.
- Track your time to understand how it is spent.
- Understand your natural productivity rhythm and choose which approach to productivity allows you to be most efficient and effective with your time.
- Set goals for the day to get the most out of the day.
- Try to focus on most important goals or tasks of the day instead of checking off many items from your to-do list.
- Consider dividing up your day into blocks of time instead of responding to requests and tasks as they come to you.
- Prepare the night before to make the following day even more productive.
- Ensure your initial schedule has some flexibility to adjust what's not working.
- Consider adding breathing space in your day to be at your most productive level

CHAPTER 17:

CREATING YOUR SCHEDULE AND SETTING BOUNDARIES

We've covered productivity, time management, and maintaining focus, but it's hard to do those things if you don't have a structure for your schedule in place. You want a schedule that helps you be at your most efficient and effective. And, boundaries are the cherry on top to keep you on task and make your valuable time even more productive.

Creating a Schedule

Being intentional with your time is incredibly important to PPWMs. For most moms I interviewed, they are the primary caregiver and want to be very specific in how they manage time daily and over the course of the week.

I asked every mom I interviewed about her schedule. Some moms swear by fewer full days, while others prefer more half-days. You want to structure your time, whichever approach you choose, so that you're at your best.

If you want to see how I specifically break down my day, check out my schedule at www.mompowerment.com. I lay out exactly how I spend my time each day of the week. And, while it might not be a perfect fit for your needs, it can help give you ideas on how to set up your own schedule.

Full Day Schedules

The moms who work fewer full days shared various ideas on what works and doesn't. For starters, childcare seems to be a lot easier to find if you work fewer full days. Several of the moms, who work full days shared that it's easier to find help, such as a nanny or babysitter. If kids are in a daycare, it still might be easier to find options because you're often charged for the full day, regardless of how long your child is at the facility. Or you might be charged a much higher price per hour to send your child half-day, so it makes sense to have a child in daycare the whole day.

These moms also talked about the ability to create boundaries between personal and professional time. If you're in the office three full days per week, then you shouldn't have to worry as much about someone grabbing you as your office time is ending or trying to get ahold of you once you've left for the day.

There are challenges with this approach. A psychotherapist in New Jersey, who works twenty-five to thirty hours per week, talked about the challenge of switching gears as the hardest part of her part-time situation. Essentially, she works one day and then is home the next day. An office manager for a construction company, who works about twenty-one hours per week in Long Island, talked about dealing with every day being different since she works every other workday. She admits that she does better with consistent structure, but working Monday, Wednesday, and Friday works better for her role at her employer.

Half-Day Schedules

On the flip side, there are moms who prefer to work more days with fewer hours. For those moms, with kids in elementary or even high school, it's probably easier to work while kids are in school. That way your boundary is pick-up time, so that you focus on kids once they're home or you're able to take kids to their afternoon activities.

These moms also talked about consistently being in the know on what's going on at the office because they were available more consistently for clients and their teams, or at least that is how it was perceived. Many entrepreneurs used this approach. Several shared that entrepreneurs must often work a little bit every day and it's hard to have the day-long breaks between work days.

As with full days, there are challenges with this approach. For those moms who need childcare, it can be hard to find childcare for a few hours every day, including daycares that don't charge you a full day for half-daycare. If you're looking for help at home, it can be hard to find a caregiver who is willing to work part-time. It depends on your situation and where you live. A self-employed designer in a small town outside of a resort in Colorado talked about the challenge of finding a caregiver, especially one who wasn't so expensive. This challenge forces her to limit the amount of business she takes on.

Boundaries at Work and at Home

You have a deadline in the next few hours and you have had countless interruptions in person, online, and via phone. Everyone knows that this is an important project and you need to get these final pieces done. Your team, manager, and your clients need to give you some space to finish.

You head home for the day to have dinner with your family or maybe you're at are at a friend's birthday happy hour. You left the office less than an hour ago and you've received several emails, calls, or texts from your team or client asking for an immediate response. Is it an emergency that needs your attention now or can it wait until you're in the office in the morning? Can't your team figure this out without you? Why can't they respect your time?

What is missing in these scenarios? There aren't boundaries. A consistent piece of advice from about 15 percent of PPWMs who I interviewed was about the need to set and maintain boundaries on the professional and personal sides.

The Boundaries at Work are Important at Home

The boundaries that you put in place at work make a huge impact on your time away from the office, especially when you're a mom and trying to spend time with your family. You want to be present with your family. If you're focused on work, especially with interruptions from your colleagues or clients, it's hard to give your family your full attention.

Be Present

When you're at home, are you thinking about work or is work outright interrupting your family time? When you're at work, do thoughts of home and family seep into your day? If you're focused on work stuff at home, you're not enjoying your time with family and friends. Chances are that if you're thinking about or being interrupted by things from home, you're not being as efficient as you can and you're also more likely to make mistakes when you're distracted.

It's important to be *present*, whether at work or at home. Figure out the infrastructure you need for home and work to make sure the other side doesn't creep into your day. There will always be emergencies, which are unavoidable, but you can make the non-emergencies stop interrupting your work or personal time.

An Austin-based OB-GYN talked about the ability to be present because of more balance in her life. She said, "It's balance dynamics. When I'm at work, I can focus 100 percent of my efforts on patients; when at home, I can focus 100 percent on my family and partner." The concept of being more present seemed a consistent theme with many moms and working part time enabled it.

For many moms I interviewed, that ability to be present enabled them to lose the mommy guilt. Since they could focus on family when they were with family, they didn't feel like work got the best of them. When they were at work, they could focus on work, knowing that they would spend time with family in a few shorts hours or for an extended period the next day.

Boundaries Can Lower Stress

Have you ever considered what stress does to you? It turns out that chronic stress, like from work or other stressors, is bad for your body. It can affect everything from digestion to sleep to the body's ability to fight infection. Your memory can start to suffer and you could start making worse decisions.[1]

Time away from the office each day helps manage stress in the short- and long-term. If you can't ever step away from work, stress levels will only go up, which is bad for us. Time away from work lets us decompress and destress. These daily or weekly moments are part of the boundaries you establish to maintain work-life balance. In addition to these small windows of time where you lower stress, consider longer stretches away from work for vacation, regardless of whether you travel somewhere or have a staycation.[2]

Time Away Enables Better Performance

Not convinced of the importance of time away? Let's talk about how time away improves your performance. You need a break each day to recharge and to perform your best. We aren't machines. We can't be productive 24/7. Our brains need to step away from work so that we're at our best.

Think about the number of times you have been working on a project for hours, days, or even months. You stop catching mistakes when you're too close to the project for extended periods of time. If you put down the project for a few hours or days, you start catching mistakes again.

That break at the end of your work day or on the weekend lets you look at your work with a fresh perspective when you start working again. In addition, it's hard to see another perspective or find the holes in your own perspective if you can't put something down for a period.

As an additional benefit, interacting with your family and friends might even trigger new ideas. I can't tell you the number of times I've been chatting with my husband at the end of the day or playing with my boys and suddenly a new idea or solution to something I've been working on pops into my head. I'm not consciously thinking about work and my brain has time to process in its own time. (That's also why I almost always have a notebook nearby.) I worked with count-less creative people in the past who talked about getting ideas in the shower or on a run. Let your mind think through something passively, while you focus on something else and it might help you as well.

Boundaries Can Help Workflow During Work Time

Boundaries also matter for getting your work done during work time. Put blocks on your calendar for different activities to be more productive with your time. Designate meeting times (some moms had designated meeting days) on your calendar so that you have desig-nated work time. Make sure your manager or senior leadership, team, and clients know about these blocks to manage their expectations and coordinate their schedules.

Consider Personal Boundaries during Work Time

We are always moms, even when we go to work. We don't get to stop being a mom during our important meetings or before a deadline. But we need to separate personal time from work. Establish what is a personal emergency. If you and your spouse both work, which is the norm these days, make sure you have a plan, whether it's day by day or weekly, on who should pick up a sick child or take a sick child to the doctor.

A financial planner in Austin, Texas, and her husband decide who will pick up a sick child and deal with any doctor appointments, based on who must cancel fewer meetings during the day. In this scenario, both parents are on equal standing, even with the mom working part-time. In this scenario, it's hard for one parent to be the daily default parent. And let's face it, that person is usually the mom.

It's important to consider this because situations come up all the time: a sick child or the nanny calls in sick, so you have to scramble for childcare. Having this discussion upfront or on whatever basis makes sense and is essential to maximizing your family's time, not just one parent's.

Financial Benefit of Boundaries

Simply stated, boundaries have a financial benefit, especially when you work part time. I have heard many times that a downfall of working part time is that you don't get paid for the all hours you work. As a director at a large accounting firm on the West Coast, who works thirty-five to forty hours, shared, "I have to be very aware of time worked or my job can have time creep and I end up working a lot more than I'm paid for." If you think about your time as money, this makes sense. If you work thirty hours per week, you should be paid for that entire time. No one wants to work for free. Boundaries can help you make sure you get paid for the time you work.

Implementing Boundaries

The easiest option is to establish boundaries from the beginning of a relationship, either a new job or with a new client. Lay these out upfront and make sure everyone agrees to the work and personal time boundaries. Establish definitions for things like emergencies or when it's appropriate for interruptions.

An event and wedding planner and transformational coach in the Chicago area shared that she sets rules and parameters from the beginning of a relationship with a client. In addition, she suggests setting a clear and concise schedule and building infrastructure around it from the beginning. For her, this includes areas such as a response time of twenty-four hours for email and phone calls. This avoids unrealistic expectations from clients and her team. This mom has set the boundary of not being available for client needs in the evening, unless there is an event she is managing. She is mom to four and wants to be present with her kids when they're all at home.

If it's an existing relationship, you might be able to put in the boundaries right away, but chances are you will need to have a period to give time for people to readjust to new boundaries and new expectations. You might need to retrain your clients, manager or senior leadership, or team when you redefine your boundaries. An option is to create a transition plan for yourself so that it's not like a light switch between two sets of boundaries. You can share the transition plan, if that makes sense, or gradually start to lengthen the response time. If you do present a plan, make sure to talk to what is changing (e.g., schedule, hours, response times to voicemail or email). You can explain how you will deal with emergencies and actually define emergencies to make your team and clients more comfortable with changes.

Boundaries When You Work at Home

Some moms talked about boundaries with family and friends, especially WFH moms. They can't simply have people stop by when kids are at school; it's their work time.

When you're working from home, you need to set the boundaries with your family. You want your family, both children and significant other, to respect your work space and your time. Establish the reasons you can be interrupted – the emergencies – or you will constantly find yourself shifting gears between things like disagreements between your children about a toy and trying to get back into work mode. My usual rule with my children is that someone needs to be hurt or it must be a situation they cannot solve. This doesn't mean situations they don't want to solve themselves. We usually go over the difference between an emergency and something they are upset about, if I have a call or a deadline. That reminder in the moment helps.

And, to be honest, I've been known to dangle a carrot for them so they know they're working toward some sort of treat, if they let me get work done, especially when I'm working toward a deadline. If you work regularly from home when your children are around, find something that works for you, with or without the reward.

Boundaries and Your Areas of Interest

A cardiologist near San Francisco, who works about thirty-five hours per week, shared that she had to provide parameters for being able to say yes. For example, "I'm very interested in the project, but I can't do anything after 4 p.m. on Tuesday or Thursday." Essentially, if the colleague or potential collaborator couldn't work with her limited availability, then the answer is no. And she had to become okay with saying no to things she found interesting.

A dentist in Austin, Texas, volunteers at her children's school every other Wednesday, which is a day she traditionally has off. When other opportunities at the school come up, she can say yes or no, based on her work schedule and the personal and professional boundaries she has long put in place.

If you struggle with saying no, you're not alone. Realize that saying "no" to something means you're saying "yes" to something else. If you're struggling with how to say no, I have a few suggestions with phrasing that I use. One of these might be helpful in your situation.

First, saying no is a full statement. You don't need to explain yourself (most of the time). And, if you do explain yourself, make it short and sweet. For example, "I can't take this on because my schedule is full right now." And that is if you feel the need to include the "because my schedule is full" part.

Second, you can say "no" without using the actual word "no." Use phrases such as "I can't right now" or "I don't have time, but thank you for thinking of me." They say "no" politely, which might feel less abrupt.

And third, if you want to say "yes" to only part of what's being asked, then do that: "I can't do X, but I can do Y at this time." Nice and simple and enables you to participate in the part you care about.

If this is for specifically something at work, a phrase I have often used is, "I can do that instead of something else I'm working on for you. What can we move around (or what deadlines can we push back or move around)?" Or something like, "I can start working on this and I'll work on the report I was already working on for you next week (or tomorrow or whatever timeframe is doable and accurate)." It reminds people that your time is limited and that you must juggle like everyone else.

If you're feeling guilty, remember that your time is one of your most important resources. You're trying to juggle a lot and make room for time with your family and for your work. Keep reminding yourself that you're saying yes to other areas in your life by saying no now. Or figure out what other things you can say no to, which are already on your plate, so that you can say yes to this.

I admit saying no is not a challenge for me. I have practiced saying no a lot and have gotten better at it over time. My own challenge in this area is that I want to say yes to several things and then I realize I have a lot more on my plate than I originally planned. I agreed when our younger son was born to not take on anything new without thinking through how it would impact all the other things I'm working on.

And I usually end up talking things through with my husband, especially if it might impact our work-life balance at home. I highly recommend you think through the impact of saying yes as it relates to all the other things on your plate and that of your significant other, and even how it might impact your family.

Putting Boundaries in Place Now

If you need ideas on how to put boundaries in place, starting now, I have a few to share.

No Technology Times at Home

Try to set times when you walk away from technology when you're at home, unless it's an emergency. And no phones at the table during meals. Use this time for family members to connect with each other and not to someone on the other end of the phone.

Response Time to Non-Emergency Communication

Look at when you respond to non-emergency communications, whether email, phone, or text. If it's always immediately, that might not be the best approach. We all want to acknowledge the people we work with, both internal and external, and be considered responsive. Ask yourself if you need to answer back with an immediate response. Probably not. Consider a new rule about non-emergency communications within twenty-four hours, by end of day, or whatever time frame you're comfortable with. Give yourself some wiggle room, so that people don't expect you to respond in minutes and then keep contacting you until you do. You could be traveling, in an all-day meeting, sick, taking care of a sick child, or working on a major deadline.

Better Define Emergency Situations

If you're running into a lot of what appears to be emergencies for your clients or team, but isn't really an emergency, it might be time to define or redefine what an emergency is. Make sure everyone agrees to those definitions, both internal like your manager and team, and external, such as clients and even vendors. Everyone you usually interact with needs to be on the same page about these definitions since they can vary from person to person or even project to project. If you need to change up the definition by project, have an initial call or summary page that everyone receives at the beginning of the project.

Tools to Help with Boundaries

You understand boundaries are important and you have some ideas of what you'd like to put in place. What about tools to help make it all come together?

Some moms suggested putting an out of office response to email and even at your desk if you work in an office and leave for several days. It's an easy way for people to know you're not available.

You can have an email response and outgoing voicemail that says you'll return the communication within a certain amount of time, such as by end of day or within twenty-four hours, which everyone agrees to ahead of time.

There are online tools you can put in place to limit your time on the internet or social media so that you can focus on work for a set time. You can lock and unlock programs or devices after a specific amount of time has passed (e.g., no internet for thirty minutes or from 10 a.m. to 12 p.m.).

There are lots of different types of tools to help with boundaries; you need to decide what kinds of boundaries will help and research the tools available. And most of them are free or have a free version.

In summary:

- Boundaries are important from a professional and personal perspective.
- Boundaries can improve your workflow.
- Having boundaries in place can help when it comes to areas of interest.
- It's important to implement boundaries the right way so they help you and aren't simply an idea.
- There is a financial benefit to boundaries so that you continue to get paid for the time you work.
- There are technical tools to help with putting boundaries in place.

PART V:
HOW PERSONAL ELEMENTS CAN HELP SET YOU UP FOR SUCCESS AS A PPWM

CASE STUDY: How to Love Your Lifestyle as a Part-Time Entrepreneur

After working about ten years in various industries and roles, a business coach for women entrepreneurs found clarity in her life and business after becoming a mother. Her journey after college started with interior design, a field in which she found quite a bit of success. It didn't seem like quite the right fit, so she kept looking at roles and industries.

She realized that she liked creating the infrastructure for businesses, such as the processes and strategies. Somewhere in the middle of all of the business stuff, she got a yoga certification and taught yoga. And then she had her first child, which helped all the pieces come together. Her mindful approach from her yoga practice married nicely with her approach to business coaching for women entrepreneurs. With a focus on family and a balanced lifestyle, she designed and structured her business to function part time. Her mindset shift was how to be professionally successful while working three days per week.

Children can help working moms prioritize and put reasonable expectations on you and your career. She gets to create the lifestyle and career she wants and can attain a six-figure salary. For this business coach, balance includes being a strong presence in her children's life.

Her advice for anyone interested in working part time:

- *Create your vision of what you're looking for.* Understand what you want out of your career. Look at what you want your schedule to be. Take time to plan out how you want the two to work together.

- *Seek outside help if you need it.* Know what kind of outside resources will actually help you and address any needs you may have. Be comfortable with asking for that help.

- *Include time for self-care.* If you're only focused on others, whether at home or work, you'll get to a point where you have nothing left to give. Build self-care time into your day, especially if you find yourself fighting burnout at work.

- *Understand what you need when you're transitioning to a part-time role.* Create support practices and make sure to build yourself up when transitioning to the part-time career approach. You want to make sure you are feeling your best when you make the transition, so you set yourself up for success.

CHAPTER 18:

MOMS NEED PERSONAL SUPPORT

About 10 percent of moms, both entrepreneurs and those who work for an employer, shared the advice of finding help. Some moms talked about help for the personal side of things, others talked about help on the professional side, and some suggested help in both areas.

Let's be honest, it can be hard to ask for help. Is that because we feel like it's a sign of weakness? Do we feel that we must be super-moms (and what does that even mean anyway)? If we're the one who others have turned to for help, do we hesitate to ask for help for our needs? Or maybe it's simply that we don't know who to ask for help?

The saying is that raising a child takes a village. Many of the moms I interviewed used this phrase, whether referring to help at home or at work. Let's talk about creating your village.

Create Your Tribe

Some people are naturally part of a tribe. Sometimes it's your actual family or even those you grew up with. Some aren't as lucky and they need to find their tribe. No question, a tribe is important. Remember what we said earlier about it takes a village? There were countless moms who I interviewed who shared they would not be able to work part time without their tribe. A lawyer in the Atlanta area said it simply, "I know my village is backing me up. I couldn't have raised my daughter and worked part-time without my village."

What do I mean by tribe, you might ask? These are people whom you have a deep connection with and are part your personal support system. They are the people we turn to, whether for help when things come up, advice, moral support, as a cheerleader to celebrate our successes, and so much more. Your tribe can include family, neighbors, friends, and your support systems (e.g., housekeeper, babysitter, or nanny). Whoever you want to include in your tribe is your decision, but make sure you have one. Don't be afraid to ask these people for help and think outside of the box.

There are times when as moms we feel like we're going through something unique when we have hard moments. That's largely because we don't usually talk about the challenges of motherhood. We want to make sure that our situation is normal and talk through daily hiccups, huge challenges, or simply get advice based on another woman or mom's experience. I can't say the number of times I asked a friend, whose kids are slightly older than mine about how to deal with a situation. And sometimes I talk to moms with kids the same age as mine to get a different perspective.

We all have our hard moments – monumental meltdowns, moments of extreme child independence, family illness, marital challenges, or even the times we feel like we're not enough as a mom, employee or entrepreneur, or as a friend. And there are so many more times when we need to be able to reach out and talk to someone in person, on the phone, or even online. It's much easier to deal with these tough moments and even the day-to-day hiccups when we have a tribe to turn to. (If you're struggling with finding your tribe, think about using the information on networking from Chapter 14 to help find like-minded people.)

What about the practical aspect of having a tribe, beyond helping you keep your sanity?

Your Tribe and Childcare

These are people you trust, so would you trust them with your children? I would trust my tribe with my children without any hesitation.

One great tip that a few moms shared in their interviews was to trade off with trusted friends and neighbors for childcare needs. Set up a schedule so that you watch your kids and hers for a time and she does the same another day. It doesn't have to be a full day of care. It can be two or three hour chunks, but that can be a lot of time to get work done without interruption. Or that might be time to exercise or take a moment for self-care, or you can even meal prep for the week without paying someone to watch your children. This approach makes sense for both moms. It's a win-win!

Know When to Ask for Help

You have a tribe of people who provide support, so now what? How else can you have a support network? In interviews, moms talked about knowing when it's time to ask for help. There were a few key reasons they knew it was time to bring in outside help.

Moms Lack Specific Skills

We are all lacking in some skills. It's normal. On the business side, maybe you aren't good at bookkeeping, social media, or even writing. On a personal note, perhaps meal planning or preparation or housekeeping is something you struggle with. There are people out there who can do each of those things. The challenge becomes finding the people who meet your needs, who you also click with, and work within your budget.

Once you figure out what you're lacking in, you need to find help in that area. Ask people you know online or off-line.

On a more personal level, online tools can help you with off-line tasks. (See an updated list on www.mompowerment.com on the Recommended Resources tab of tools I use or that moms I interviewed use.) Online resources include a virtual assistant, project management tools, or time management tools, to name a few. These are predominantly online needs or ones that can be filled virtually. Ask for recommendations, interview people, and compare options, just as you would with off-line options. These types of resources can be integral to building a business as an entrepreneur or keeping you sane when you have an employer. Even if you can't afford a lot of someone's time, even a few hours of a service can help fuel growth in your business or get tasks done (e.g., birthday party stuff, coordinating teacher gifts, etc.).

Tasks Are Too Time Consuming

Is there something that takes up a lot of time proportionate to your overall schedule? Again, meal preparation or maybe housekeeping might be one of these areas. Either you need to figure out how to be more efficient with these tasks or it might be time to consider outside help. There are lots of aspects of maintaining your home that you can outsource. And it doesn't need to be a professional service that you turn to for help. There might even neighborhood kids who are looking to make more money for things like yard service. A mother's helper can tidy up after the kids, which can sometimes feel like a full-time job (well, at least in my house with our two young boys).

Sometimes we can turn to our significant other or a family member, but that's not always an option. When my husband and I are both at our busiest times of the year, I might ask for a mother's helper to come one or two times a week late in the day to heat up dinner and sit with our boys while they eat, and help get them ready for bed. The other five or six nights we're eating dinner as a family, but those one or two nights, my husband and I are getting more done. It helps keep stress levels down. And after the boys are ready for bed and have heard a few stories, either my husband or I tuck them in. This can be a teenager in the neighborhood or a sitter we use regularly. I've even had a housekeeper come to only clean bathrooms, change sheets, and mop the floor. It's an hour, but that would have taken me hours of my time when I could be working. And it's a limited time during the year, so it's not cost prohibitive.

From a business perspective, especially as an entrepreneur, are there areas that take up a lot of your time in comparison to all the other work you do? For example, if your strength is business strategy, does social media take up a lot of your time because you must figure out all aspects of social media, find or create the right content, etc.? Perhaps you need to put people and systems in place to make things more efficient.

If you struggle with paying the money, consider how much money you might be losing by focusing on these tasks that take up more time than they would if someone else worked on them. You might be saying that you don't want to pay that money because you don't have the money. Let's consider the financials. For this example, you pay someone $15 per hour to do something and you get paid $60 per hour. Essentially, you're losing money by doing dishes or finding content for your Twitter feed. In this example, you could be losing more than $4600 each year if you do two hours of work each week on these tasks versus having someone else do it ($60*2*52 week versus $15*2*52 week). You could lose thousands of dollars each year by taking on all these tasks that are time consuming that don't necessarily add value to your day and take away from time with your family, career, or business.

You Dread Household or Work Duties

Is there something you cannot stand doing, even if you know how and even it's not that much time? For example, many moms I spoke with hire a housekeeper to come to their homes once a week or month. They realized that even with more time, housekeeping was still something they didn't want to do. A branding strategist in Cody, Wyoming, who works about twenty hours per week, shared that she doesn't enjoy meal planning, but that her sister is a caterer, and does the meal plan and the meal prep once groceries are purchased. Many moms I know can't stand grocery shopping, which can also be time consuming. They have meals delivered, use services that plan meals and send the ingredients already portioned out, or buy groceries through an online service. There are all kinds of services in these categories, so you have options.

On the professional side, moms shared they use a bookkeeper to send out invoices and chase down money. There are people who focus on all sorts of aspects of business that can help you: Facebook ads, social media, bookkeeping, marketing, financial strategy, and research. The list is endless. You must find the right resources for your needs, so that your money is used most effectively for your situation. And you can add services over time, based on changes in your business or an increased budget.

In summary:

Creating a support network is important to PPWMs.

- Your tribe, whoever that includes, is important, especially when you work part time.
- Asking for help is still important when you're a PPWM. You need to understand when and who to ask for help and support.
- Consider help at home and with your work needs.

CHAPTER 19:

PPWM AND SELF-CARE

Take Care of Yourself

Some of you who are reading this might be really good at taking care of yourself, including eating well, exercising, and getting enough sleep. If you're like most moms, taking care of yourself falls off the to-do list regularly.

Taking better care of yourself includes making healthier food choices. I won't turn this into a lecture on eating well, but I will remind you that what you eat fuels you or it simply fills you up. When you're fueling your body, you likely feel better and are more energized, right? Find ways to have a breakfast that fills you up. You want to have lunch options that are healthy and that you enjoy. Take time to figure those options out and actually include them in your diet (and by diet I mean eating habit and not your attempt at losing weight). And while you're at it with trying to eat healthier, don't forget to drink enough water throughout the day.

Slow down and take time to eat. Yes, several moms I interviewed eat lunch at their desk, but that still means they can enjoy what they're eating. And, so can you. You don't have make it a five-course meal, but you can enjoy the short (or long) time you have.

I understand how busy you are, but you still need exercise and sleep. I'm going to talk about exercise a bit differently than a trainer or fitness coach. I'm coming at this from the perspective of a busy, working mom, like you.

When it comes to exercise, I'm sure we all know that exercising three, four, or, yes, seven, days a week for thirty minutes or more each day is ideal. I understand that. I also understand that can be hard. So, instead of skipping your thirty-minute workout because you can't fit it all in, try a different approach. It's something I started at the beginning of this year. I exercise whenever and for however long I can. It can add up to thirty minutes throughout the day. Or if it doesn't, fifteen minutes is better than nothing. And, if I fit in longer stretches, that's great! And if not, I let the short bursts of exercise add up.

And don't forget to sleep. At some point, refueling yourself requires sleep – turning everything off and getting into bed to let your body recoup. I won't say it must be a certain number of hours, but work on getting the right amount of sleep for your own needs.

Your Self-care Routine

We will spend the time doing what's necessary for our kids, significant other, parents, neighbors, volunteering obligations, etc., but what about spending time on ourselves? So many of the moms I interviewed talked about the need as a PPWM to take time for self-care. Their message is clear – we need to make time to fill our cups. Self-care makes each of us be a better mom, significant other, friend, sibling, colleague, neighbor, you name it.

How can we be at our best when we often turn away from taking care of ourselves? It might even sound counterintuitive, but think about it. How can we take care of others with our full energy and be present if we're not at our best? And that is mental, physical, emotional – a holistic version of – care. As one mom describes it, "I'm happier and it trickles down to my kids, who are also happier."

It doesn't have to be a visit to the spa, unless that is what you want. I'm referring to self-care as a consistent part of life, so that we don't feel drained over time and unhappy with ourselves and those around us. By that point, it can be harder to be present and happy with our families and our work.

So how can we bring self-care into our day when we're so busy? The answer to that is very personal. It's what you need, not what your sister, friend, neighbor, or anyone else needs. Remember, we're not trying to be perfect; we're trying to be our best self. That's all we can ask for, right? Here are a few things to consider when you're figuring out your self-care routine:

- What makes you happy, outside of family and potentially work stuff? What is it about that thing that makes you happy? How else does it make you feel (e.g., light, fun, calm, energized, etc.)?
- Is there an activity that makes you smile, even just thinking about it? What is it about that activity that you enjoy?
- Can you think of an image that gets you to think happy thoughts? Where are you? What are you doing?
- What's something you can do to help you integrate small moments of self-care in your day or week?
- What can you do to integrate big moments of self-care into your day or week?
- What's one thing that immediately changes your mood (e.g., dancing, laughing, etc.)?
- When you think of relaxing or filling your cup, what does that look like?

I've given ideas for figuring out what fills your cup, but really, it can be anything – a nap, writing in a journal, meditation, reading a book, taking a walk or a short hike in nature, lunch or happy hour with a friend, talking on the phone with a friend you haven't spent time with in a while, taking a bubble bath, gardening, or even something more luxurious like a spa outing. Anything that helps fill your cup can be part of your self-care routine. And the way we want to fill our cup can vary from day to day or even throughout the day.

You might say you don't have time for self-care on a regular basis, so try something once a week. Or consider rethinking what you do for self-care daily. I do a morning check-in with myself before I even get out of bed. I see how I'm feeling. For example, if I'm tired, I may need to give myself more time to get things done (and not press the snooze button) or maybe take something off my to-do list that isn't necessary today. Maybe I'm feeling stressed because of looming deadlines, so I know to breathe more. Even when I'm super excited about something, I know it can impact my family if they aren't feeling that same excitement. It's a small thing, but it makes a difference for me and those I've suggested it to.

Another simple thing is taking deep breaths. We're not talking heavy breathing. I'm talking breaths from your diaphragm. It only takes a few minutes of deep breaths to get the benefit.

If you're more visual, create something like an inspiration board with images of you doing things you love. Maybe you have pictures from a recent trip somewhere that you really enjoyed. Include a few snapshots of places you visited or want to visit. Let your mind wander and enjoy the moment. Imagine yourself there. You don't have to have an entire inspiration board. It can even be a picture or two that allows you to find that happy moment.

And, as much as I think it's important to find simple moments of self-care each day, you shouldn't hesitate to take a day or two or ten for your self-care, if that's what you need. That means getting away from the day-to-day obligations and family. Maybe it will be more fun with a good friend or in a group. The idea is to enjoy the day or weekend or week, letting everything else fall away. And, again, make it what you want and need. Figure out how to fill your cup and do that thing.

Keep in mind that these are ideas and you might have something that's already working for you. Do whatever is right for your own needs and make sure to integrate a bit of that into your week and, I hope, into your day.

What's Stopping You?

I've shared why it's important to include self-care in your routine, especially as a busy, working mom. And even how to figure out what you can do for self-care, if you don't know already. I gave examples and even shared my own self-care rituals, some of which only take minutes.

So, here's my question to you. What's stopping you from integrating self-care into your day or week? Is it not enough time? Do you need to use your time better? Can you make adjustments in your to-do list such as delegating? Are there things you can remove from your list, because some things don't have to get done today or this week? Are you simply trying to do too much in a day and setting an unreasonable expectation of your time?

Are you limiting your definition of self-care? Remember, you don't need hours, so see how you might be able to fit small moments of self-care into your busy day. If you want to go big, schedule it on your calendar and make sure nothing gets in the way of that self-care day or week.

Are you not sure if it's worth your time or if you have earned it? I can tell you already that it is and that you've more than earned it. Mama, let me remind you that you're doing your best. And you deserve a moment to yourself. Honestly, you deserve hours and days for your self-care, but moments are likely what you can fit in to your busy life. Put it on the calendar if that's what it takes.

Take that moment to fill your cup. Take as many moments as you need and want to fill your cup. You want it. You need it. You've earned it. Enjoy it!

In summary:

We all need self-care as part of our usual routine.
- Make healthy food choices and drink water.

- Exercise and get enough sleep.
- If you don't already know how to fill your cup, explore different ways to do this.
- Schedule your self-care moments into your day if you need to.

CHAPTER 20:

MANAGING MOMMY GUILT

A TOPIC THAT COMES up time and time again in my conversations with moms and in a few interviews is mommy guilt. I will admit that mommy guilt is not something that I personally struggle with. I understand that most moms deal with it, sometimes daily or even several times a day. I don't judge the moms who feel its pull and I hope they don't judge me.

There are three things that seems to keep my mommy guilt at bay. First, our initial experience with school for our older son (and subsequently for our younger son) has been amazing. Second, working part time gives me the work-life balance I need. And finally, my working part time is all our boys have ever known, which has helped manage expectations on all sides.

What Does Your Child Need?

When our older son was about fifteen months old, we took him with us to look at mothers' day out programs (essentially half-day preschool for younger kids), so that I could have more consistent time to work. He thought it was amazing that there was a place with kid-sized stuff and toys everywhere. He loved the idea of playing with classmates his age every day he went to school. For us, the challenge was that he didn't want to leave and we had to wait about four months to come back for the start of his school year.

When his school finally started that fall, he was eighteen months old. He was so excited that first day that he walked into the classroom without even giving me a hug or saying goodbye. The other nine children in his class were crying and he walked in and started playing. I was sad for about a minute until the teacher whispered to me, "You need to leave right now," as she attempted to keep our son smiling, while consoling nine other unhappy children with the help of her teacher's aide.

I might have felt more guilt over time if his teacher wouldn't have been like another grandmother, providing such a loving environment and teaching our older son new skills. My theory is that his continued enthusiasm about school and learning is largely because of the amazing experiences he had from the very beginning, spending Tuesdays and Thursdays with his loving teachers, 9 a.m.-1:30 p.m.

He continued to have amazing teachers, who he adored, throughout preschool. He loves to learn and take it all in like a sponge. And he is very social and talks about the interactions with friends and all the fun stuff they're doing. Keeping him out of school would have been unkind on my part. I wouldn't have been able to mimic that learning and social environment at home, even with playdates and teaching him new things. His preschool teachers provided activities that I wouldn't have come up with on my own.

We found out how incredibly enthusiastic he is about school when he started kindergarten in fall 2016. The first few weeks of school, he was waking up at 4:45 or 5 each morning. That went on for the first two or three weeks because he was that excited about going to school. The added challenge was that he was waking up our then almost three-year old. It's a long day when you've been up since 4:45 a.m. with two young children. I finally had to sit him down and explain that school doesn't open at 5 a.m. or even 6 a.m. and that he might not be able to learn as much as his classmates if he is too tired. Thankfully, that worked. Let's hope this passion for school continues.

We're taking the same path with our younger son, who also loves school so far. He talks about his teachers and the activities he does in class. He asks about his teachers and classmates on the weekends. It's amazing to watch. I won't lie, it's wonderful to know that you leave your child in the hands of teachers they adore, who are loving and enthusiastic with the kids they teach. I know we're fortunate and that has helped remove any guilt I might have felt if things were different. I might have abandoned my part-time professional opportunities if my boys were crying every day at drop-off. But, thankfully that's not the case.

Since I know my children and their enthusiasm about school, I don't feel guilty about their time at school. I decided that my kids' needs include going to school and that is good for them and for me.

How can you use this? Think through what your child needs. If he or she is having fun, learning, and enjoying the school or daycare experience, isn't that what's important? Maybe that can help minimize some of your mommy guilt.

What Do You Need?

On the flip side, it's helpful to consider your needs. I need to work to keep my sanity. I am a go-getter and am very goal-oriented. Setting goals related to work and achieving them is important to me. I need work to counter-balance my family life. I'm not willing to work full time because I want time with my boys, but I do want to work. I don't feel guilt for wanting this balance between career and family.

I'm not alone in feeling this way. A mom in event sales in Atlanta, who works five to twenty hours a week, described the situation perfectly: "Some moms are made to be SAHMs and some are made to work outside of the home. I need a break and I need social interaction with adults." And this is key. This mom knows herself and knows what she needs and embraces it.

A Chicago-based language expert who works fifteen to twenty hours each week teaching young children and adults, described her approach as, "Don't let guilt 'haunt' you." She encourages moms to understand their professional needs and feel empowered to make decisions based on those needs.

If you want or need to work, whether for personal or even financial reasons, be at peace with that. You are still likely spending a lot of time with your kids when they aren't in school. You're still making the effort to have the work-life balance that you need and that's all you can ask of yourself.

There are times when I need to jump on a call or finish one final thing for a client after I've grabbed my boys from school. I don't do this regularly, but, when I do, I don't feel guilty about it. I spend a lot of time with our boys most weeks – almost forty hours a week.

Take a moment to understand what you need versus what your family needs. If you want to spend time with your child, but it's a busy time, take a fifteen- or thirty-minute break to focus on your child. Get down on the floor and play and enjoy the moment. I find that focused time with my boys can make a huge difference for both me and my boys. Don't feel guilty because of your break from work though, because it's something you need or your child needs in that moment.

I would think about it differently if I let playtime or time with my boys regularly take my entire work day or if I worked every day, when I had set aside time with my boys. It's reasonable to do this on occasion without bringing guilt into the mix.

Start Working Part-time When They're Young

The one final thing I will share that helps with managing mommy guilt is that I started working part-time early on as a mother. My working part-time is all my boys have ever known. Even working for a large company for the first year, on my short days, I was back early enough to play in the afternoon with our older son. Two days a week, it was the two of us, doing fun stuff or simply hanging out.

When I started working for myself a year after our older son was born, I began my work-from-home journey. Our younger son has only experienced life with mom working at home part time. And we started him in the baby room, where his older brother was attending preschool, when he was ten months old.

I am usually the face that greets them at the end of their day. I understand that I am fortunate to work for myself from home and have flexibility. I can volunteer at their schools or attend special events like a class party. I get to spend hours with them each afternoon, hanging out, playing outside, or letting them make me dinner in their play kitchen. We have time to read books and build LEGOS.

Can Moms Have It All?

The moms who I know in my network, including those who I interviewed, seem to be harder on themselves than they are on others. As moms and even as women, we often have high expectations of ourselves. We are told that we can have it all when we're young and as we go through college. This concept is hard to maintain over time and puts a lot of pressure on us. And, honestly, we put a lot of pressure on ourselves to have it all. And not only to have it all, but to be amazing in all things all the time. If you focus too much on perfection in your own situation, you will feel disappointed because it's hard to be consistently perfect all the time. It's also exhausting to deal with this all day every day. Who has enough energy to keep that up? I certainly don't. Do you?

It's Personal

For most of the moms I spoke with and in my own case, it's important to understand your own situation and to figure out what works for you and your family. It's very personal and it's largely about your individual perspective and needs, both professionally and personally. Take the time to think through what will work in your situation for you and your family. Leave the guilt out of the equation and be comfortable with the decisions you make for your career, family, and the balance in between.

Don't Compare Yourself to the Joneses

If you focus on what others are doing, whether SAHMs, or FT-WMs, or even other part-time working moms, you will likely feel guilty about your approach or about what you're not doing right. In part, that guilt might be driven by feelings of not doing enough, especially in an age when we see so much perfection on Facebook, Pinterest, and Instagram. Don't compare your situation to others, because each situation is different and you never know what the next mom isn't focusing energy on that you are. And who knows what happened a few minutes before and after the perfect moment you see online or in a holiday card, or hear about at the PTA meeting. And, from what I see with other moms, the more you compare to other moms and family situations, the more likely you are to feel guilty.

Give Yourself Some Grace

As much pressure as we might put on ourselves, we must remember to be kind and give ourselves some grace when it's not perfect, because some moments, days, or even weeks won't be. Own your strengths and be comfortable with "good enough." If you feel the need to be amazing in all areas of your life all the time, be kind to yourself if that doesn't happen.

Change the Definition

If you feel you must have it all, maybe it's time to change the definition of "having it all." Make the definition of what success looks like to you a personal one and include the pieces you find most important. Again, don't compare to others or use their definition. Don't look at your friends, colleagues, or what a magazine or book says. Only you know what's most important to you and your family. You get to define, create your terms, and set your priorities. And, it's not something you set and it stays consistent, so allow for some flexibility. You have the flexibility and the permission to redefine these over time, because it can all change.

Besides, guilt might transform over time. A media director, who works about twenty hours per week at a large marketing agency in Austin, Texas, shared she felt guilty because she wanted to get involved with her children's activities as they got older and she couldn't turn off the office. She felt the need to make an adjustment because she wanted to be a better wife and mother, so she transitioned to a part-time role. She still deals with guilt, but now it's when she's not at the office and feels like she might be missing something at work.

Mommy Guilt in the Interviews

An Austin-based make-up artist, who works ten to twenty-five hours a week, shared that she feels mommy guilt because she might miss her children's activities due to work. Her schedule is known months in advance, and kids' events get scheduled after the work calendar is already set. She doesn't want to disappoint her kids and have them feel she doesn't support what they're doing.

An office manager for a landscaping business in Long Island, New York, who works twenty hours a week, shared she has mommy guilt for doing chores on the two days when she's home with her younger son. Instead of doing fun stuff with her younger child while her older children are at school, she needs to get things done, so that weekends are freed up to do fun stuff as a family. Ultimately, she is using her non-working days to benefit her family, but it still affects her younger son and that makes her feel guilty.

The owner of an advertising and marketing business in Austin, Texas, who works about thirty hours a week, feels a "bit of guilt because she is always connected, since she needs to be accessible by her clients." She is always available to clients, but she isn't always working. She feels guilty for being connected and for the times when she does have to work.

These might be similar to your own situation. What can you do to feel less guilty about your own situation? Can you put more boundaries in place? Can you better define what is an appropriate reason for your team or a client to reach out after hours? Is there a way you can set expectations with your child for the times when you do have to work for a bit when you would usually play? What might help to decrease the guilt that you might feel when you must stay connected, even when you work part-time?

The most common reason for mommy guilt in the interviews was when things had to change unexpectedly, usually for a unique work situation. I understand that this can be tough for a child to understand. I remind moms, though, that when you usually spend twenty or even forty hours with your child each week, those unusual situations are OK. Sure, they are inconvenient for you and your family, but they aren't usually going to break everything you've built in your work-life balance.

In summary:

Managing mommy guilt is made easier by:
- Understanding your needs and those of your family
- Redefining what having it all means
- Not comparing your own situation to anyone else's
- Being kind to yourself when things are out of balance

PART VI:
DEALING WITH CHALLENGES AS A PPWM

CASE STUDY: Design a Life in Which You Can Make Adjustments

This branding expert lives away from a large city and enjoys every aspect of her life. An artist at an early age, she had a mentor and teacher help her grow her artistic skills. She has since taught herself about how to design and create brands, learning the software by playing around at her father's architectural firm. And now she marries her artistic ability with her understanding of branding, using the tools she has learned and mastered over time.

She started out as a reluctant entrepreneur after seeing the sometimes-stressful lifestyle of owning a business that her own parents had. Over time her business evolved from selling her artwork to now helping brands create what they stand for visually. Her business kicked into high gear once she learned through a coach and virtual coursework how to run a business. And now the designer and branding expert is collaborating with her husband, an expert in all things audio and video, so they work as a team.

She describes their life as "very editable," so she and her husband make adjustments along the path. She does work she loves about twenty to twenty-five hours per week and has lots of time with her family. On Tuesday through Friday, the branding expert works from about 10 a.m. to 2 p.m. and then when the kids are in bed. She doesn't work on Mondays. She has been able to create her work schedule to match the needs of her family. She and her husband are creating the life they want on their terms.

Her advice for anyone interested in working part time:

- *Live frugally.* Live within your means and you can make adjustments without being as concerned about the impact.

- *Divide household and parental duties equally.* Enable each partner to do his or her share.

- *Work doing something you love.* Essentially, figure out how to monetize the things you love to do and it won't feel like work.

- *Acknowledge areas you're not good at and ask for help.* Her sister, a caterer, does meal planning and even helps translate that to grocery lists.

- *Find the right tools.* The designer specifically mentioned Trello, a project management application, as a tool that helps her in her business. She suggests finding whatever tools you need and that work for you. You want to figure out what will make you more efficient and productive in your work and at home.

CHAPTER 21:

PPWMS SHARE THEIR
CHALLENGES AND SOLUTIONS

THIS BOOK IS LARGELY about how to set yourself up for success. Along the way, I've included stories of how other moms have thrived to give you ideas and help you along your own path. And while I like to focus on the positive, I would be remiss if I didn't mention that being a PPWM has its challenges.

As much as transitioning to a professional part-time role helps moms achieve their work-life balance and make things easier, it doesn't necessarily make things easy. Let's look at some of those challenges and potential ways to overcome the roadblocks you face as a PPWM.

Being More Productive in Less Time

Going from a full-time role, often in a demanding industry for many of the moms I interviewed, to a part-time role required a shift in mindset. For some moms, they needed to reset expectations on what they would or could achieve in less time.

When a business coach in Philadelphia, who now works about twenty hours per week, became a mom, she used that moment to figure out her business. She decided after the birth of her daughter that she needed to figure out her coaching business or become a SAHM. The business coach describes motherhood as giving her "strength" and "clarity" when it came to understanding what her coaching business needed to look like and who she wanted to serve. And then she needed to understand what she could accomplish during her work week. Her biggest challenge was that she, "had to get into the headspace of having a successful business in twenty hours per week."

Her solution was that she gets to her "zone of genius" more quickly, which means she must be more intentional with her time. The business coach redefined what she offers, which allowed her to combine what she learned from her yoga certification about mindfulness with strategic business building. She made decisions to find help with things like housekeeping duties, because that didn't add value to her business or roles as mother and wife, but they still need to be done. And finally, she prioritizes what she wants to accomplish on her three-day weekly schedule.

Professional Challenges

Professional challenges came up again and again as something moms needed to find solutions for. Many moms, in general, talked about the need for an adjustment period to overcome challenges. As you start to consider your own transition understanding these challenges and the work-arounds might be helpful in your situation.

Great Efficiency, but Limited Growth

A few moms I interviewed talked about not learning new things once they started working part time. One mom, who works thirty to thirty-five hours per week as legal counsel for a large technology company in Austin, Texas, described her situation as her "duties are frozen in time, where her skills and knowledge aren't really increasing." Essentially, instead of growing her knowledge and skills and taking on new tasks and projects, she's becoming more efficient at her job over time.

It is important to become more productive at work over time, whether you work full time or part time, but learning new skills is also important. This might be an area you negotiate with your manager or senior leadership. Consider, for example, including something in your written proposal that you attend a specific number of trainings each year. Or include something about exposure to new project or concepts over the course of the year, so that you keep learning new things and growing your skill set, even while working part time.

What Happens When You're Overqualified

Several moms talked about being overqualified for their current role, whether they were entrepreneurs working with clients or for an employer. You want a role that allows for flexibility and fully utilizes your skills, but you might also want to work on projects that make you stretch professionally.

Some moms talked about their managers, especially when on a new team or at a new company, not understanding what moms could handle in less time. As a chemical engineer in a petrochemical company, who works about twenty hours per week, explained, "Managers don't always know how to handle part-time workers. You might have to help him or her understand your perspective and workload and [skills]." And know that this lack of understanding about part-time employees might also mean that you have to say no to some projects if your workload is maxed out.

Remember that you can always ask for more work or more challenging work, but it's hard to ask for less. You'll never look bad if you ask for more work and even bring opportunities to your manager for projects you can take on. You can essentially work with your manager to figure out a path on which you continue to grow professionally.

The same solutions apply to clients if you're an entrepreneur. You still need to do the work you've been hired to do, but will it hurt to talk to your client about making your role more efficient and using more of your skills? Is there a new project you can recommend, where you can push your own skills and get results for your client(s)?

Managing the Type-A Drive When You Work Part Time

How do you manage a Type-A personality when you transition to a professional part-time role? This is a challenge I heard from moms who described themselves as high performers, before and after going part time.

If you've been a go-to person who is used to achieving and making things happen, how do you turn that off? A Denver-based senior software engineer, who works about thirty hours per week, describes it as learning to "do less work." Her solution has two parts. She admits that she has changed how she looks at her career: "I'm not looking to climb the ladder; I'm looking to do a good job." And, from a personal perspective, she's focusing on family, making sure to be less hurried when spending time with her girls.

A director at a consulting firm, who works about twenty hours per week, explained that she needed to figure out how to add value in her new capacity. That took time and effort, although it was helpful that she had years of history with the company and with her manager to help with that. And she admits, "My trajectory has flattened, but I can take a step back and get gratification in raising my kids." Her perspective has shifted, at least for now, in her journey as a mother who also wants to have a demanding career.

"My struggle is how to keep the [creative] spark alive while being a mom." The music teacher and performer, who works about fifteen to twenty hour each week, in Orlando, Florida, shares her challenge and solution. She changed her focus and her perspective to that of "there will be other work opportunities and things will happen again [in her career], but kids' stuff won't." She has been able to mix in some performances in recent years, but her main focus is her family. The music teacher and performer talks about having to shift her perspective to be satisfied with her current approach to performing.

Financial Challenges

I shared early on in this book that 59 percent of moms didn't feel that having a child had impacted their career path, according to a Pew Research Study.[1] It turns out that there is mommy bias, according to research done by Cornell University. There is about a five percent per child wage gap on top of the idea that moms are less committed after having children.[2] And less commitment can lead to fewer promotions and financial implications, such as even lower pay increases and/or bonuses.[3]

In general, the financial side of the equation was one of the topics was most often mentioned as a negative of working part time. Not all moms shared their income information, but, of those that did, about half make the same as an average full-time worker in the United States and worked less than the standard forty-hour work week (average in my research was about twenty-four hours per week).

One of the most important ways to combat the potential financial challenges is to understand your value. Especially if you're a seasoned employee (in experience and/or time with a company), you bring skills, knowledge, and know-how to the table. It can be expensive for a company to find those things in a new employee and it can take time.[4] Remember not to focus on the reduction in salary when you're starting the conversation about reducing hours, at least not in the initial stages of your discussion.

Challenges Around Household and Child Duties

Sharing Household and Child Duties with your Significant Other

One of the topics I haven't spoken about is the need for more sharing of household and parental duties among parents, so that it's not moms who must do these things. While this needs to happen, it will take time for a shift in mindset in most households. Many of the moms I spoke with – more than 75 percent – have the lion's share of household and parental responsibility. Especially in the households where moms continue to have a demanding career, even part time, this can be a sticking point among couples.

One of the ways an engineer at a petrochemical company, who works thirty-two hours per week, has dealt with this challenge is to hire someone who is part nanny, housekeeper, and household manager to do the things that neither parent can get to. It has made their household function more efficiently, as you can imagine. And, everything gets done and both parents can continue to have their demanding careers. And the engineer's time after work and on the weekend is spent enjoying time with her kids and husband instead of doing all the household things that must be done.

As I shared, one of the top five recommendations from moms was to find help. And it happens that finding help with household duties was a top tip. See what you need, whether it's a housekeeper or nanny, or some combination, and find that person. Be specific in what you want that person to do when you're in the hiring process.

If you need help with these areas, but think that financially it's not feasible, see if some parts may be. Maybe even having someone come for an hour every few weeks will help deal with an element of household chores like cleaning bathrooms or mopping, which you don't want to deal with.

Have an open and honest discussion with your significant other about dividing up duties. Some moms I talked to had a significant other who does all or most of the cooking for the family. Or the dads do drop off in the morning, so that moms can hit the ground running as soon as kids are out of the house or get to work earlier. In my household, whoever does dishes doesn't put the kids down. See where there are opportunities for your significant other to help out regularly. My biggest piece of advice is being specific with what you need from your significant other, especially if you want it done your way, or be comfortable with it being done and not necessarily your way.

And, let's be honest, the challenge of childcare is something many families struggle with, whether both parents work full time or in the situations where one works part time and the other full time. It can be costly and challenging to find the right childcare. For most families, childcare is expensive in comparison to overall income. The think tank, New America, collaborated with Care.com on a program to understand childcare and the growing costs. They found that in the United States, the average cost of childcare per child in childcare centers for ages newborn to four is $9,589 per year as of 2016.[5] Keep in mind that the average annual cost of in-state college tuition is $9,410.[6] According to the report, "the cost of full-time care in child care centers is 85 percent of the monthly U.S. median cost of rent".[7] Essentially, the cost of childcare compares to both college tuition and rent. How can all families afford it?

With those high costs in mind, don't forget to use your support network to come up with creative solutions such as working playdates or switch off with another mom you trust, so each of you has time to work.

Motherhood Is Different When You Work Part Time

While talking to a friend who now works part time, she shared that she didn't realize what she was in for when it came to being around her children for more of the day. Yes, you'll get to spend a lot more time with your kids, which is amazing, but you'll also see a lot more of all aspects of your children.

I'm referring to interacting more with their energy shifts (we all have highs and lows), natural intensity, a fuller range of their emotions, and more of the small and big changes that happen each day. For some moms, this can be overwhelming and exhausting initially. A mom shared that it took a year to figure out how to take care of her kids part time, when she had been working full time for years.

The moms who talked about this suggested giving yourself time to adjust. They also shared that moms should take a moment to step away from the overwhelm if they need to. Find a way for everyone to deal with stress (e.g., dance party, laugh, get everyone to read during a ten- to fifteen-minute "break," or even simply hug it out). You can always try to talk it out (not interrogate) to see what is creating these intense emotions, actions, etc. And, finally, don't forget to practice self-care.

Logistical Challenges

When You Can't Add More into Your Schedule

Logistics can be unbelievably challenging to deal with when you have children. Professionally, logistics can include not being able to work with some clients or accommodate others when you have a part-time schedule.

A hair stylist in Austin, Texas, who works about thirty-five hours per week, shared that she can't be flexible with clients because her hours are based on her daughter's elementary school schedule. Most clients do understand her situation as she has long history with the vast majority of them. She is as flexible as she can be and is understanding when a client moves to another stylist. She has also tried to open up a Saturday each month to accommodate clients who can't come during her normal hours.

Consider Commuting Time in your Overall Schedule

A few moms shared that their full-time schedules became too much after a move, when their commute times made their overall schedules too hard with kids. They wouldn't have seen their kids awake until the weekend. As they were planning their transition and setting up their schedule, they still needed to factor in this element so that it was manageable. Commute time is something that must be considered when it comes to working part time. If your child attends school 8 a.m.-2:30 p.m., that might not mean you can work that whole time, especially if you have a long commute. Consider your commute time and make sure to analyze how a potential move can make your time in the car shorter or longer. It could be the difference between keeping the job and walking away.

As a potential way to offset your commute time, figure out how to make use of the time. Schedule calls or standing meetings with your team while you're in the car. It's a great time to do check-ins, although you want to do some of these in person as well where you can look at your team member or manager in the eyes and read non-verbal cues. This might impact the number of days you work or even if you negotiate a work-from-home situation one day per week.

Future Challenges

What If It Doesn't Work Out?

Two moms I spoke with shared that a professional part-time role simply didn't work for them. A former engineer at a Houston-based international petrochemical company shared that she had two very different part-time experiences. The first was fine and she worked four days per week. The second part-time experience ultimately led to her leaving the company. She seemed to get more less desirable projects and roles after transitioning to a part-time role the second time. When her mother passed away, she reassessed what she wanted and being a SAHM was ultimately her goal.

A former accountant in Omaha, Nebraska, had been out of the workforce for twelve years when she reentered. After working about eighteen months, the company was asking for more and more of her time. When the hours started to affect her family's life, she realized the increase wasn't working for her. Her former employer needed someone to be available more than she could be, so they parted ways. She decided that would focus on family again for a time and reassess her needs again later.

Ultimately, a part-time role might not be for everyone. It might be that your employer isn't supportive or doesn't understand how to fully utilize your limited time. It could be that your needs have changed. Whatever has happened, it's reasonable to transition to what does work for your family. That might be a SAHM or FTWM situation. If you're still interested in the PPWM role, consider it when circumstances, professional or personal, have changed.

What's Next?

An attorney, who has her own practice part time for the past ten years shared, "I have a lot of legal experience, but I don't really fit into a traditional situation anymore." If at some point she wants to return to work for a firm, it will likely be hard to figure out what she could do within the structure of a typical law firm. She understood that when she decided to work part time for herself, and she understood the repercussions of it in her career.

If you're concerned about future opportunities, moms provided suggestions in two areas. First, understand your motivation and timing. Maybe you want to spend time with your kids for a few years and then go back to work. Keep this in mind from the beginning and let it guide your decisions. And second, understand the difference between going part time at an employer and becoming an entrepreneur. Can you transition to part time with your current employer? Are you able to hit the ground running with clients or do you have to ramp up as an entrepreneur? Does one better align with your long-term needs? Figure out how to make the better option work, even if it's harder initially.

You've Transitioned to a Professional Part-time Role, Then What?

About 26 percent shared that they either will or probably will go back to work full time (some even have since being interviewed). What happens when you've decided that you want to head back to work full-time after you've been working part time for a few months or even years?

As with changing to a part-time role, moving back to a full-time role is a transition and one that shouldn't be done overnight. Take time to understand the feasibility, opportunity, and the pros and cons of the transition (back) to full time for your own situation. Looks at both career and personal implications. Break them all down and you'll know if full time is right for you.

If you're not sure if this full time (or heading back to full time) is the right move for you, these questions might help you think through the decision:

Career Questions about Transition Back to Full Time

- Is there a full-time position available for your skills and level of expertise at your current employer or will you be looking for a job with another company (or starting your own business)?
- Does the full-time salary meet your expectations?
- Are there specific benefits you might want to negotiate, even if you plan on working with the same company where you work now, even in your same role but with full-time hours?
- If you're changing roles because they don't have budget for a full-time person in your current role, do you need to update your skills or do training? If so, how will that work? Who will pay for it? How will you transition from your current role to the full-time role? Do you need to transition someone to your current role? How can you balance the two needs?

- What is the timing of the transition?
- What changes, if any, will you deal with regarding benefits (e.g., vacation time or even health and dental benefits)? When will those changes take effect?
- What happens if you get pregnant and want to go part time again? Does timing matter?
- How does this fit into your long-term career trajectory and overall plan?
- Can you gradually transition back to full time, so that it's not like a light switch?

Questions about the Personal Side of Transition Back to Full Time

- What is your motivation for this transition? Essentially, what is driving the interest in going back to work full time?
- What is your childcare plan when you transition back to full time? How quickly can this be put in place? How does that align in the timing for the transition to the full-time role?
- Will going back to work full time impact any of your child's activities? If so, how? If there is an effect, has that been discussed with your child? If this is an area your child is passionate about, can you hire someone to help with pick up and/or drop off so he or she gets to continue to participate?
- Will you need flexibility from your employer (or client) when you're in this full-time role? This might help you understand if you need to transition to a flexible job that's full time versus a normal full-time role.
- Do you have any concerns about the timing (e.g., can you get all your ducks in a row regarding childcare or after school care, etc.)?

These initial questions can get you thinking about your transition back to full time. They can get you thinking about your plan and next steps.

If you're excited about the prospect about transitioning to or back to full time, keep moving toward your goal. Even if things aren't perfect, it's still a doable situation and professional working moms do it every day. Make sure it's the right move for the right reason though. Understand the impact on you and your family. If you're comfortable with those changes, make it happen. You can do it!

If you're not comfortable with the current plan, what can you do to feel more sure of the changes you want? How will you make those changes happen? Unless there is an outside influence driving you, you likely have a choice. Maybe consider this isn't the right transition or right time for the transition. You can look at the transition back to full time in a few months or a year or even a few years. Take time to find the right position at the right company. It's worth it. And keep building your network, however slow and with whatever level of effort you can, because you never know where that ideal full-time role might come from.

If you continue to work part time, don't question that. It's quite common among the moms I interviewed, with 43 percent continuing or highly likely to continue in a part-time role. Keep networking with people inside and outside of your employer. Continue to grow your area of expertise and your knowledge base, however slow that happens and with whatever level of effort you're able to maintain. You never know when you might have the career spark ignited by something or someone new. And don't forget that the future might look different than you expected initially. A transformational coach in the Dallas area shares her thought on being open to change as you move forward: "Pivot when necessary and give yourself permission to modify or adjust."

In summary:

Working part time can give you more of what you want in your life, but it's not necessarily easy. There are challenges that PPWMs face, which they must overcome. During the interviews, moms shared challenges which fall into five categories:

- Increasing productivity
- Professional challenges
- Household and childcare duties
- Logistical challenges
- How to deal with the future

FINAL THOUGHTS

I ASKED YOU INITIALLY to consider what is holding you back in making a shift in your career approach. And now, I hope you answer, "Nothing is holding me back." And, if you still hear those voices of doubt, start breaking down the challenges and answering the questions you have. Be confident in your path. Know your strengths and your value as an employee or entrepreneur. And remember, that nothing will happen if you don't look for and ask for the change you want. The answer is always no if you don't even ask the question.

I wrote this book to empower moms with knowledge and tools to think differently about their career approach and to make changes happen. I've shared stories from PPWMs in all sorts of industries across the United States, showing this is doable in all sorts of fields. And I've shared tips and advice from the amazing women who shared their stories with me.

You are not alone in your interest in making this change. And, chances are, that if you work at a large company, there are probably other moms who are asking these same questions around the same time you are. What if you went to management as a group and started talking about changes in work-life balance instead of having one-off conversations with managers or senior leadership, with each mom negotiating individually? Think about the power of larger groups in negotiating, influencing, and driving change, instead of the power of one.

You might be the first mom at your employer who wants to make changes in her career approach. Start the conversations with your manager and senior leadership. Start asking the questions and start sharing answers. Begin the path and lead the way; don't shy away because you're first. Help employers provide you with support as you figure out and articulate what you want and need. Someone must lead the way. Maybe that person is you in this case.

If you're the first mom to make this transition at a small or big company, talk to other moms about your experience, successes, and challenges. Lead the path and show how you made the transition happen. Share your ups and downs and advice. Provide direction to your employer. Be a trailblazer and embrace that you can open doors for other moms behind you.

If you decide that entrepreneurship is your path, feel empowered to take on clients who understand your version of work-life balance. Be confident in your skills and knowledge and know that will attract the right clients, in the short and/or long-term. Build your business and don't get discouraged. I always tell my boys when we're doing something tough, "Slow and steady." Build your business how you want and be secure in your decision.

Pay it forward. Mentor and sponsor women that follow your path, so that they don't have to struggle the way you might have. Hire moms and workers who want to work part time. Enable your own team to think differently about their career approach and support the path they choose with your efforts.

And, if you're an employer who couldn't create more flexibility so you had seasoned and strong employees leave to start their own business, what about using their services? They know your company and understand your needs intimately. They could be incredibly productive freelancers or consultants who you can tap in to. Show them that they aren't alone in their endeavor to find work-life balance.

If we stopped considering ourselves alone on this journey and came together as a group, we are more likely to make major shifts happen. If we share with others about our own journey, we empower each other with information, which leads to more moms feeling that they have options. We need the message to be clear that moms don't have to choose between career and family if they don't want to. We must start the conversations and the change will become inevitable.

ACKNOWLEDGEMENTS

WRITING THIS BOOK SIMPLY wouldn't have been possible without the more than 110 professional part-time working moms sharing their stories. I cannot say thank you enough to the women who gave me an intimate glimpse into their lives and shared their advice and insights.

There were several women who read and shared their opinion on content, flow, and overall ideas. To Alexa Bigwarfe and Lisa Carlson, thank you for taking time to read the book early on and letting me know your thoughts. Alexa, thank you for your guidance and professional help along this journey. Valerie Anderson, you went above and beyond with your initial read of this book. I can't say thank you enough.

To Holly Edger, you helped me think through the initial idea of Mompowerment and took the time to give feedback to make it a better book. I appreciate all you did and am so glad to call you friend.

A special thank you to Emily Kapit. I'm also so glad that our paths crossed early on this journey. Your input on the book helped create the resource that it is. I appreciate your perspective and insights always. I'm forever thankful for our mutual accountability and our friendship.

Thank you to Lilah Higgins, branding and designer extraordinaire, and Katie Zupan, the talented illustrator, for taking my initial unfocused thoughts and creating an amazing cover.

I want to give a special thanks to my editor Betsy Rhame-Minor. Thank you for clarifying my ideas and always answering my questions. You are truly a pleasure to work with.

To my parents, thank you for being so supportive over the past few years. I appreciate all you do for us always.

My wonderful husband Robert has been so supportive during this endeavor. I love you oodles. I appreciate your endless encouragement on this journey and the countless hours of IT help. Thank you for always saying that I could do anything, regardless of what was ahead. And I'm so thankful for your stellar kitchen skills!

To my boys, A&E, I love you to the moon and back. Thank you for keeping life interesting and giving me a spectacular reason to want more work-life balance. I love my time with you, especially our local and far off adventures. Here's to many more new and exciting adventures in our future.

END NOTES

Introduction

1 Lisa Belkin, "The Opt-Out Revolution," The New York Times Magazine, October 26, 2003, http://www.nytimes.com/2003/10/26/magazine/the-opt-out-revolution.html.

2 Judith Warner, "The Opt-Out Generation Wants Back In," The New York Times, August 7, 2013, http://www.nytimes.com/2013/08/11/magazine/the-opt-out-generation-wants-back-in.html?_r=0.

Chapter 1

1 Wendy Wang. "Mothers and Work: What's 'Ideal'?", Fact Tank: News in the Numbers, Pew Research, Washington, D.C., http://www.pewresearch.org/fact-tank/2013/08/19/mothers-and-work-whats-ideal/.

2 Ibid.

3 U.S. Department of Labor, "Happy Mother's Day from BLS: Working Mothers in 2012," The Economics Daily, U.S. Bureau of Statistics, May 10, 2013, https://www.bls.gov/opub/ted/2013/ted_20130510.htm.

Chapter 2

1 Kenneth Mathos, Ellen Galinsky, and James T. Bond, National Study of Employers (Alexandria, VA: Society for Human Resource Management, 2016) 23, http://whenworkworks.org/downloads/2016-National-Study-of-Employers.pdf.

2 Ibid., 26.

3 Chris Weller, "These 10 Countries Have the Best Parental Leave Policies in the World," Business Insider, August 22, 2013, http://www.businessinsider.com/countries-with-best-parental-leave-2016-8/.

4   Center on the Developing Child, "Five Numbers to Remember about Early Childhood Development (Brief)," Center on the Developing Child, 2009, http://developingchild.harvard.edu/resources/five-numbers-to-remember-about-early-childhood-development/.

5   Ibid.

6   D'Vera Cohn and Paul Taylor, "Baby Boomers Approach 65 – Glumly," Pew Research Center: Social and Demographic Trends, Washington, D.C., December 20, 2010, http://www.pewsocialtrends.org/2010/12/20/baby-boomers-approach-65-glumly.

7   Gretchen Livingston, "For Most Highly Educated Women, Motherhood Doesn't Start until the 30s," Fact Tank: News in the Numbers, Pew Research Center, Washington, D.C., January 15, 2015, http://www.pewresearch.org/fact-tank/2015/01/15/for-most-highly-educated-women-motherhood-doesnt-start-until-the-30s/.

8   "Fast Facts about Fertility," Resolve: The National Fertility Association, April 9, 2015, http://www.resolve.org/about/fast-facts-about-fertility.html.

9   "Raising Kids and Running a Household: How Working Parents Share the Load," Pew Research Center: Social and Demographic Trends, Washington, D.C., November 4, 2015, http://www.pewsocialtrends.org/2015/11/04/raising-kids-and-running-a-household-how-working-parents-share-the-load/.

Chapter 3

1   Nikki Graf, "Most Americans Say Children Are Better Off with a Parent at Home," Fact Tank: News in the Numbers, Pew Research Center, Washington, D.C., October 10, 2016, http://www.pewresearch.org/fact-tank/2016/10/10/most-americans-say-children-are-better-off-with-a-parent-at-home/.

2   Working Mother Research Institute, Breadwinning Moms: The Working Mother Report (New York, NY: Bonner Corporation, 2016), 4, http://www.workingmother.com/sites/workingmother.com/files/

attachments/2016/04/breadwinningmoms.pdf.

3   Kathleen L. McGinn, Mayra Ruiz Castro, and Elizabeth Long Lingo, "Mums the Word! Cross-national Effects of Maternal Employment on Gender Inequalities at Work and at Home," Harvard Business School Working Paper, No. 15-094, June 2015, (Revised July 2015): 19-20,

https://dash.harvard.edu/bitstream/handle/1/16727933/15-094%20(2).pdf?sequence=4.

4   Ibid., 18.

5   Ibid., 18-19.

6   Ibid., 20.

7   Ibid., 28.

8   W. Bradford Wilcox, "Moms Who Cut Back at Work Are Happier," The Atlantic, December 18, 2013, https://www.theatlantic.com/business/archive/2013/12/moms-who-cut-back-at-work-are-happier/282460/.

9   Pew Research Center, "Raising Kids and Running a Household: How Working Parents Share the Load.

Chapter 4

1   PL+US: Paid Leave for the United States, "Forging Ahead or Falling Behind? Paid Family Leave at America's Top Companies," Paid Leave for the United States, November 16, 2016, https://d3n8a8pro7vhmx.cloudfront.net/plus/pages/48/attachments/original/1480616519/report.pdf?1480616519.

2   "Family," PWC/United States, 2015-2017, http://www.pwc.com/us/en/about-us/diversity/pwc-family-support.html.

3   Rachel Gillett, "20 Great Places for Moms to Work," Business Insider, June 15, 2015, http://www.businessinsider.com/the-best-places-for-new-moms-to-work-2015-6.

4   Ariane Hegewisch and Emma Williams-Baron, "The Gender Wage Gap by Occupation and by Race and Ethnicity," Institute for

Women's Policy Research, 2017, https://iwpr.org/issue/employment-education-economic-change/pay-equity-discrimination/.

Chapter 7

1   United States Department of Labor Bureau of Labor Statistics, "Employer Costs for Employee Compensation News Release Text," United States Department of Labor, March 17, 2017. https://www.bls.gov/news.release/ecec.nr0.htm.

Chapter 8

1   United States Small Business Administration Office of Advocacy, "Small Business Profile," The Small Business Advocate 35, no. 1 (March-April 2016): 3, https://www.sba.gov/sites/default/files/March_April_2016_FINAL_508_compliant.pdf.

2   Ibid.

3   Arnobio Morelix, Victor Hwang, and Inara S. Tareque, State of Entrepreneurship 2017. Zero Barriers: Three Mega Trends Sharing Future of Entrepreneurship (Kansas City, MO: Ewing Marion Kauffman Foundation, 2017), 9, http://www.kauffman.org/~/media/kauffman_org/resources/2017/state_of_entrepreneurship_address_report_2017.pdf.

4   Womenable, "The 2016 State of Women-Owned Business Report," American Express OPEN, April 2016, http://about.americanexpress.com/news/docs/2016x/2016SWOB.pdf.

5   Ibid.

6   First Round Capital, First Round 10-year project, n.d., accessed April 4, 2017, http://10years.firstround.com/.

7   Marisa LaScala, "It's Small Business Week – Remember the Mompreneurs," Working Mother, May 5, 2015, http://www.workingmother.com/content/small-business-week-remember-mompreneurs.

8   First Round Capital, First Round 10-year project.

Chapter 9

1   Gallup, State of American Workplace (Gallup, Inc., 2017), 153, accessed April 4, 2017, http://www.gallup.com/reports/199961/state-american-workplace-report-2017.aspx.

Chapter 10

1   D'Vera Cohn and Paul Taylor, "Baby Boomers Approach 65 – Glumly."

2   James Manyika , Michael Chui, Mehdi Miremadi, Jacques Bughin, Katy George, Paul Willmott, and Martin Dewhurst, McKinsey Global Institute, A future that works: Automation, Employment, and Productivity (McKinsey Global Institute, January 2017), 82, http://www.mckinsey.com/global-themes/digital-disruption/harnessing-automation-for-a-future-that-works.

3   Ibid., 33.

4   PriceWaterhouseCoopers, Millennials at Work: Reshaping the Workplace (New York, NY: PriceWaterhouseCoopers, 2011), 8, accessed June 15, 2017, http://www.pwc.com/gx/en/managing-tomorrows-people/future-of-work/assets/reshaping-the-workplace.pdf.

5   Teresa Meek, "Work/Life Balance: What It Means to Millennials," Coca-Cola Journey, October 1, 2014, http://www.coca-colacompany.com/stories/work-life-balance-what-it-means-to-millennials.

6   Ibid.

7   Jacquelyn Smith, "13 Things Successful Millennials Do in Their Spare Time," Business Insider, July 24, 2014, http://www.businessinsider.com/successful-millennials-spare-time-2014-7.

8   Richard Fry, "Millennials Surpass Gen Xers as the Largest Generation in U.S. Labor Force," Fact Tank: News in Numbers, Pew Research Center, Washington, D.C., May 11, 2015, http://www.pewresearch.org/fact-tank/2015/05/11/millennials-surpass-gen-xers-as-the-largest-generation-in-u-s-labor-force/.

9   Lisa Rabasca Roepe, "Are Gen X Women Being Squeezed Out of the Workplace?," Fast Company, December 15, 2015, https://www.fastcompany.com/3054410/are-gen-x-women-being-squeezed-out-of-the-workplace.

10   Ibid.

11   Ibid.

12   Ibid.

13   Ibid.

14   "Generation X 101," BridgeWorks, February 21, 2017, http://www.generations.com/2017/02/21/genration-x-101/.

15   Ibid.

16   Ibid.

17   Ibid.

18   Lisa Rabasca Roepe, "Are Gen X Women Being Squeezed Out of the Workplace?".

19   The Sage Group, Survey Report: 2015 Sage State of the Startup (Irvine, CA: The Sage Group, 2015), https://www.sage.com/na/~/media/site/sagena/responsive/docs/startup/report.

20   "Generation X 101," BridgeWorks.

Chapter 11

1   Marcus Noland and Tyler Moran, "Study: Firms with More Women in the C-Suite Are More Profitable," Harvard Business Review, February 8, 2016, https://hbr.org/2016/02/study-firms-with-more-women-in-the-c-suite-are-more-profitable.

2   Julie Kantor and A. Crosser, "High Turnover Costs Way More Than You Think," The Huffington Post, February 11, 2017, http://www.huffingtonpost.com/julie-kantor/high-turnover-costs-way-more-than-you-think_b_9197238.html.

3   Ibid.

Chapter 13

1   Sylvia Ann Hewlett, "The Right Way to Find a Career Sponsor," Harvard Business Review, September 11, 2013, https://hbr.org/2013/09/the-right-way-to-find-a-career-sponsor.

2   Sava Berhané, "Why Women Need Career Sponsors More Than Mentors," Fast Company, August 28, 2015, https://www.fastcompany.com/3050430/why-women-need-career-sponsors-more-than-mentors.

3   Geri Stengel, "Sponsorship: Why Entrepreneurs Should Take a Page from the Corporate Playbook," Forbes, June 12, 2013, https://www.forbes.com/sites/geristengel/2013/06/12/sponsorship-why-entrepreneurs-should-take-a-page-from-the-corporate-playbook.

4   Ibid.

5   Ibid.

6   Sava Berhané, "Why Women Need Career Sponsors More Than Mentors."

7   Sylvia Ann Hewlett, "Make Yourself Sponsor-Worthy," Harvard Business Review, February 6, 2014, https://hbr.org/2014/02/make-yourself-sponsor-worthy.

8   Ibid.

9   Ibid.

Chapter 16

1   Shana Lebowitz, "Here's How the 40-Hour Workweek Became the Standard in America," Business Insider, October 24, 2015, http://www.businessinsider.com/history-of-the-40-hour-workweek-2015-10.

2   Ibid.

3   Douglas Brinkley, "The 40-hour Revolution," Time, March 31, 2003, http://content.time.com/time/specials/packages/article/0,28804,1977881_1977883_1977922,00.html.

4   Joe Myers, "Why Scientists Think We Should Be Working 3-Day Weeks," World Economic Forum, April 16, 2016, https://www.weforum.org/agenda/2016/04/why-scientists-think-we-should-be-

working-three-day-weeks/.

5   Joe Robinson, "The Secret to Increased Productivity: Taking Time Off," Entrepreneur, October 2014, www.entrepreneur.com/article/237446 (accessed from Forbes.com June 17, 2017).

6   Herb Axilrod, "4 Methods to Increase Employee Productivity," Entrepreneur, April 29, 2015, https://www.entrepreneur.com/article/245644.

7   Leigh Buchanan, "Why This Company Thrives on the 5-Hour Workday," Inc., October 9, 2015, http://www.inc.com/leigh-buchanan/stephan-aarstol-why-this-company-thrives-on-5-hour-workday.html.

8   Stephen Aarstol, "What Happened When I Moved My Company To A 5-Hour Workday," Fast Company, August 30, 2016, https://www.fastcompany.com/3063262/what-happened-when-i-moved-my-company-to-a-5-hour-workday.

9   Laura Vanderkam, "14 Time Management Strategies from Highly Productive People," Laura Vanderkam, January 22, 2016, http://lauravanderkam.com/2016/01/14-time-management-strategies-from-highly-productive-people/.

10   Tucker Cummings, "The Pomodoro Technique: Is it Right for You?", Lifehack accessed June 17, 2017, http://www.lifehack.org/articles/productivity/the-pomodoro-technique-is-it-right-for-you.html.

11   Laura Vanderkam, "Manage Your Time," Laura Vanderkam, 2017, http://lauravanderkam.com/books/168-hours/manage-your-time/.

12   Ibid.

13   Dana Malstaff, Nurture Your Business: How I Run My Business When I'm Overwhelmed and Under Water, Episode 105, podcast audio, BossMom, August 26, 2016, https://boss-mom.com/episode-105-nurture-your-business-how-i-run-my-business-when-im-overwhlemed-and-under-water-with-dana-podcast/.

14   Ibid.

Chapter 17

1   Susan Krauss Whitbourne, "The importance of vacations to our physical and mental health," Psychology Today, June 22, 2010, https://www.psychologytoday.com/blog/fulfillment-any-age/201006/the-importance-vacations-our-physical-and-mental-health.

2   Ibid.

Chapter 21

1   Pew Research Center, "Raising Kids and Running a Household: How Working Parents Share the Load."

2   Shelley J. Correll, Stephen Bernard, and In Paik, "Getting a Job: Is There a Motherhood Penalty?" American Journal of Sociology 112, no. 5 (March 2007): 1297–1339, http://gender.stanford.edu/sites/default/files/motherhoodpenalty.pdf.

3   Ibid.

4   Julie Kantor and A. Crosser, "High Turnover Costs Way More Than You Think."

5   Brigid Schulte and Alieza Durana, The New America Care Report (Washington, D.C.:, New America, 2016), 5, accessed September 28, 2016, https://www.newamerica.org/better-life-lab/policy-papers/new-america-care-report/.

6   Ibid.

7   Ibid.

ABOUT THE AUTHOR

Suzanne Brown is a part-time strategic marketing and business consultant, TEDx speaker, author, and avid international traveler. For more than 12 years, Suzanne worked at various large marketing agencies in Austin, New York, Miami, Chicago, and San Antonio, managing integrated marketing campaigns for large international corporate clients.

While still at a large marketing agency, her part-time work story started, after the birth of her older son.

Suzanne started her entrepreneurial venture after having a consulting side business for 7 years while still in the corporate world. As a consultant with her own clients, she had more flexibility and control over her schedule. A year into being an entrepreneur, Suzanne realized that there were limited resources for career moms interested in transitioning to a professional part-time role. And the idea for her book was born.

Suzanne received her MBA, Bachelor of Business Administration, and Bachelor of Arts in Spanish from The University of Texas at Austin. Suzanne and her husband live in Austin, Texas. You can often find them during non-work time trying to keep up with their two active young boys, whether on a local hike or a far-off adventure.

Read more from Suzanne about topics related to being a busy, working mom and find more resources and templates to help you on your own professional part-time journey at www.mompowerment. com.

Made in the USA
San Bernardino, CA
13 March 2018